"Estate planning libraries abound with books on tax savings and financial management. But very, very few provide practical guidance about the human experience of being an heir. **ROTTENBERG GIVES EXCELLENT ADVICE ABOUT HOW TO PARTICIPATE PROACTIVELY BUT RESPECTFULLY IN YOUR PARENTS' ESTATE PLANNING**, how to face realistically the financial consequences of a parent's death, and how to behave responsibly as a beneficiary of unearned wealth. **ALL THIS WITH INSIGHT, COMPASSION, AND REMARKABLE ACCURACY.**"

> GERALD LE VAN
> Managing Director
> The Le Van Company
> Author of *The Survival Guide for Business Families*

". . . **HOW WONDERFUL TO FIND SUCH A PRAGMATIC AND EMOTIONALLY ACCURATE GUIDE TO THE TRICKY PROCESS OF WEALTH TRANSFER.** I especially appreciate this book's emphasis on the value of philanthropy; sharing their resources is, without a doubt, the most healing and empowering thing heirs can do."

> KATHERINE GIBSON
> Cofounder
> The Inheritance Project

"There are many books on death and taxes, but Dan Rottenberg's **INTERESTING, REAL LIFE ANECDOTES SHOULD PROVE EXTREMELY VALUABLE IN HELPING READERS**. . . take the appropriate estate planning action."

> CHARLES K. PLOTNICK, ESQ.
> Plotnick & Ellis and coauthor of *How to Settle an Estate: A Manual for Executors and Trustees*

THE
Inheritor's
HANDBOOK

Also available from
BLOOMBERG PRESS

Investing in REITs:
Real Estate Investment Trusts
by Ralph L. Block

Smart Questions to Ask Your Financial Advisers
by Lynn Brenner

Staying Wealthy:
Strategies for Protecting Your Assets
by Brian H. Breuel

Investing in Small-Cap Stocks
by Christopher Graja and Elizabeth Ungar, Ph.D.

Investing in Hedge Funds
by Joseph G. Nicholas
(January 1999)

Kids and Money:
Giving Them the Savvy to Succeed Financially
by Jayne A. Pearl

The New Commonsense Guide to Mutual Funds
by Mary Rowland

A Commonsense Guide to Your 401(k)
by Mary Rowland

BLOOMBERG PERSONAL BOOKSHELF

THE
Inheritor's
HANDBOOK

A Definitive Guide for Beneficiaries

DAN ROTTENBERG

BLOOMBERG PRESS
PRINCETON

Books are available for bulk purchases at special discounts. Special editions or book excerpts can also be created to specifications. For information, please write: Special Markets Department, Bloomberg Press.

This publication contains the author's opinions and is designed to provide accurate and authoritative information. It is sold with the understanding that the author, publisher, and Bloomberg L.P. are not engaged in rendering legal, accounting, investment-planning, or other professional advice. The reader should seek the services of a qualified professional for such advice; the author, publisher, and Bloomberg L.P. cannot be held responsible for any loss incurred as a result of specific investments or planning decisions made by the reader.

First edition published 1999
    3 5 7 9 10 8 6 4 2

Rottenberg, Dan.
    The inheritor's handbook / Dan Rottenberg. – – 1st ed.
        p.   cm. – – (Bloomberg personal bookshelf)
    Includes index.
    ISBN 1-57660-051-3
    1. Inheritance and succession- -United States- -Popular works.
I. Title. II. Series.
KF750.Z9R677   1999
346.7305'2- -dc21   98-34093
                                                             CIP

Acquired and edited by Steven Gittelson

Book design by Don Morris Design

To Barbara

PART 2

When Wealth Changes Hands   84

PART 3

Handling New Wealth **120**

ACKNOWLEDGMENTS

THE REASON THE WORLD is so confused, I've often observed, is that the experts can't communicate and the communicators don't know anything. As a professional communicator—specifically, a journalist—I couldn't have written this book without the insights, advice, and encouragement of literally dozens of experts in fields related to inheritance. I list them here not only to thank them for their help but also to personally vouch for their capabilities to readers in need of professional advice.

This book grew out of articles I wrote on trusts for *Bloomberg Personal Finance* magazine. The idea for such a book was first suggested by my editors at Bloomberg, Steven Gittelson and Jared Kieling, to whom I am grateful not only for that perception but also for the astute manner in which they shepherded the book through to publication. Thanks are due also to my agent Louise Quayle for handling all the contractual details and thus allowing me to focus on research details.

Even before the book was envisioned, the catalyst for my magazine article on trusts was Standish H. Smith, the founder and driving force behind Heirs Inc., the Villanova, Pennsylvania–based support group for trust beneficiaries. He and Norman E. Donoghue II, a Philadelphia estate lawyer, gave especially generously of their time and expertise, even reviewing the book's manuscript.

Others who offered information and insights include:

LAWYERS: Lawrence Barth (Philadelphia), James Bartles (Palm Beach, Florida), Richard Bishop (Greenfield, Massachusetts), Dominic Campisi (San Francisco), Richard D. Greenfield (Ardmore, Pennsylvania), Michael Harris (Plymouth Meeting, Pennsylvania), Howard W. Harrison Jr. (Villanova, Pennsylvania),

Gregory Harvey (Philadelphia), Gregory B. Jordan (Pittsburgh), Michael B. McGovern (Washington, D.C.), Gordon A. Millspaugh (Warren, New Jersey), Charles Plotnick (Jenkintown, Pennsylvania), Robert Whitman (University of Connecticut).

FINANCIAL PLANNERS: Carole Badger (National Association of Personal Financial Advisors, Buffalo Grove, Illinois), Tom Batterman (Wausau, Wisconsin), Stan Breitbard (Los Angeles), Cynthia D. Coddington (Cambridge, Massachusetts), David Diesslin (Fort Worth, Texas), Dr. Jeffrey Feldman (Rochester, New York), Nancy Frank (New York City), Melissa Hammel (Brentwood, Tennessee), Martha Kapouch (West Hartford, Connecticut), Deena Katz (Coral Gables, Florida), Brent Kessel (Santa Monica, California), Tim Kochis (San Francisco), Dee Lee (Harvard, Massachusetts), Warren Mackensen (Hampton, New Hampshire), Steve Mintz (Monroe, Louisiana), Charles L. Parker Jr. (Houston), Raj Pillai (Solon, Ohio), Myra Salzer (Boulder, Colorado), Barbara Steinmetz (Burlingame, California).

PSYCHOLOGISTS AND THERAPISTS: John L. Levy (Mill Valley, California), SaraKay Smullens (Philadelphia).

OTHER COUNSELORS: Tracy Gary (San Francisco), Gerald Le Van (Charlotte, North Carolina), Rob Rikoon (Santa Fe, New Mexico).

BANKERS AND TRUST OFFICERS: Sonia Barbara (American Bankers Association, Washington), Donald J. Danilek (Bank of Bermuda, New York), Jim Dever (Mellon Bank), Bradford Greer (Cypress Trust, Palm Beach, Florida), Jan Lessman (Pennsylvania Bankers Association, Harrisburg), J. David Officer (Mellon Bank), Daniel Reisteter (Pennsylvania Bankers Association, Harrisburg), David R. Schwartz (Glenmede Trust Co., Philadelphia), Angela Yarbrough (Pennsylvania Bankers Association, Harrisburg).

FINANCIAL JOURNALISTS: Allen Hancock (*More Than Money*, Arlington, Massachusetts), Mary Rowland (Rhinebeck, New York).

INHERITORS WHO SHARED THEIR PERSONAL STORIES WITH ME INCLUDE: Rick Adams (New York), Michael Alexander (Toronto), Barbara Blouin (Halifax, Nova Scotia), Mel Fingerut (Sarasota, Florida), Bernard Freedman (Philadelphia), Katherine Gibson (Blacksburg, Virginia), Martha Greene (Greenfield, Massachusetts), Sally Lowell (Brockton, Massachusetts), Gary R. Marbut (Missoula, Montana), Suzanne McCormick (Dobbs Ferry, New York), Herman Moore (Charlotte, North Carolina), and John Upp (Cecilton, Maryland).

DAN ROTTENBERG

INTRODUCTION

OU AND I HAVE never met, but already I know the single most important fact about you: You, your parents, and your spouse will die one day.

The death of a parent or spouse is often a shattering experience, for two reasons: first, because you lose forever a primary source of love and emotional support; and second, because precisely at this moment when you're most emotionally vulnerable, you may need to make critical financial decisions.

When you pause to think about it, these can be terrifying prospects. So terrifying, in fact, that most people *refuse* to think about them. As a result, the tragedy of death is often compounded into financial catastrophe. When your parent or spouse dies, he or she won't feel the consequences—but you will.

If you're a survivor or a potential survivor, what can you do? Until now, most experts have assumed that you could do very little—because technically, what your parents do with their estate is none of your business. Mom and Dad can leave all they have—or none of it—to you, and they don't even have to tell you what they decide. If they leave the estate to you in trust, that's traditionally none of your business, either: The trustee, not you, is in charge of the assets.

For these reasons, dozens of guidebooks have been written to help men and women write their wills and plan their estates. But inheritors—whose needs may be far greater, and whose powers are far fewer—have had few places to turn for help. This book seeks to fill that void—whether the need arises before the death of your parents or spouse, at the time of death, or years after the death. It seeks to help inheritors and potential inheritors avoid unnecessary suffering and *additional* loss when a loved one dies.

10 BASIC RULES

FOR STARTERS, here are 10 basic rules that should serve you in good stead until you've digested the rest of this book:

1 Dealing with an estate—before or after death— is important. Even if your family's estate is modest, your failure (or your family's failure) to pay attention to it can cause considerable pain and expense to you and your relatives. It can mean that decisions about your family's property will be made by strangers in courts or in corporate bureaucracies. It can mean your parents' or spouse's property will be disposed of in a manner they never intended.

2 It's not that important. Estate and inheritance matters shouldn't be ignored, but neither should they consume you. Money and property *per se* don't buy happiness or solve problems; they merely provide greater opportunity to become happy or miserable, depending on your nature. Too many happy families have been torn apart by legal fights over inheritance. Maintain your perspective: Your ultimate goal is a happy, healthy, and rewarding life. A material inheritance may be a means to achieve that end, but it's not the end in itself.

3 Ninety percent of the problems you encounter after your parents (or spouse) die can be eliminated by talking to them about death and money before they die. This book offers practical advice about doing just that. If you can't talk to your parents about death and money (and don't feel bad— most of us are in the same boat), or if you're already an inheritor, this book will, of course, address your situation as well.

4 Seek good advice. In the long run, a few hundred (or even a few thousand) dollars for a good lawyer, accountant, or financial adviser is money very well spent.

5 No expert or book has all the answers. You know your parents better than anyone—

including me. Do your homework but make your plans based on your unique knowledge of your family's unique situation.

6 The biggest obstacles you'll encounter as an heir will be emotional matters, not financial ones. Many problems that appear on the surface to be financial—like jockeying for assets or income with your siblings, trustees, and lawyers— actually stem from emotional roots. To tackle your inheritance issues in a pragmatic fashion, you probably need good therapists or family counselors as much as you need good lawyers and financial planners.

7 Prepare yourself not only for your parents' death, but for their incapacity. Dealing with Alzheimer's disease, stroke, caregivers, and nursing homes may be more exhausting and expensive than dealing with death and estate issues.

8 If you've inherited more money than you need, develop a serious approach to philanthropy. This serves not only the worthy causes you fund but your own needs as well—by reducing your tax burden and, more important, by providing you and your inheritance with a sense of worthiness.

   9 **Find meaningful work for yourself, even if you don't need to work for a living.** As Camus put it: "Without work, all life goes rotten. But when work is soulless, life stifles and dies."

10 **Whatever you do, do it sooner rather than later.** Death rarely arrives at a convenient or predictable time. Be prepared. A will can always be changed while its author is still alive. It can't be changed once its author has died.

HOW TO USE THIS BOOK

YOU DON'T HAVE to read this book from start to finish. It will serve you best if you focus on the stage you've reached in the inheritance process. For example:

◆ If your parents or spouse are still living, concentrate on **PART 1**; doing so will make your life infinitely easier after they die—so much easier, in fact, that you may be able to skip Parts 2 and 3 altogether.

◆ If your parents or spouse have just died, jump to **PART 2**, which discusses what you need to do at the time of death and in the months that follow.

◆ If the death occurred years ago, and you have questions or problems about the way things have turned out—for example, if you're the beneficiary of a trust and you're unhappy with the trustee's performance—skip Parts 1 and 2 and proceed directly to **PART 3**.

Whichever section you consult, use the glossary at the back of the book to look up terms you don't understand. You'll also find other helpful resources and information there.

Above all, throughout this book you'll find practical advice and good examples of famous and ordinary people who've walked in your shoes. You'll find useful names, addresses, and phone numbers. And you'll find comfort.

THANKS TO AWESOME breakthroughs in biotechnology, surgical techniques, and DNA research, some medical scientists believe that the human life span could be doubled or tripled by the end of the 21st century, thereby postponing the inevitability of death or even eliminating death altogether. Unfortunately, you and I won't be around to find out if that happens. For the foreseeable future, we must make the most of the only life we have. One of the best ways of doing that is by dealing sensibly with death. By confronting death with the proper knowledge and preparation, you can make the best of an essential and inevitable human transition. Regardless of the dollars involved, dealing maturely with loved ones about life's most sensitive issues can be one of life's most rewarding experiences.

DAN ROTTENBERG
Philadelphia
May 1998

TWO NOTES ABOUT STYLE

◆ For the sake of clarity and smooth reading, most of the text is addressed to a son or daughter who is about to inherit or has already inherited assets from his or her parents. But, of course, virtually all the advice conveyed in this book also applies to husbands or wives who inherit from their spouses. If that's your situation, simply substitute the phrase *your spouse* wherever the book refers to *your parents.*

◆ Also for the sake of clarity, the book avoids unwieldy all-inclusive gender pronouns like "he or she" and "his or her." Instead, I just use one or the other. Obviously, an heir can be either male or female, and so can a stockbroker, a lawyer, an accountant, a spouse, a parent, or a child.

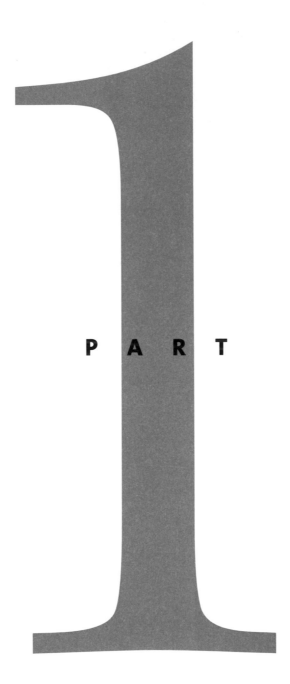

PART

Preparing to INHERIT

RNOLD BERNHARD was a stock-picking genius who founded Value Line, Inc. in 1931, built it into the nation's largest investment advisory service, and ran it until he died in 1987 at the age of 86. But when it came to managing his own family's affairs, this shrewd adviser could have used some advice himself.

Two years before he died, Bernhard set up a family trust and bequeathed to his daughter, Jean Buttner, two more shares of Value Line stock than he gave her twin brother, Van. By this tactic, Arnold Bernhard assured Jean's control of the company—and also placed Van in the humiliating position of needing court permission to extricate his part of the family business from his sister's control. As children, Jean and Van spoke the special language of twins; but until a court decision in 1996 forced Jean to buy out Van's stake, they reportedly communicated with each other only through their lawyers.

The Bernhard family's sad schism begs an obvious question: If the financially astute Arnold Bernhard couldn't arrange a stress-free transfer of his wealth, what hope is there for the rest of us? The answer seems to be that making fortunes and arranging for their transfer may well require two very different types of brainpower. As the Sears Roebuck heir Lessing Rosenwald famously put it, "It is easier to make $1 million than to give it away wisely."

YOUR RELATIONSHIP WITH YOUR PARENTS

IF YOU'RE AN adult with living parents, sooner or later you'll face the inevitable day when your parents die and you must cope with their estate.

Today's tax laws, notes Warren, New Jersey, tax lawyer Gordon Millspaugh, all but guarantee that "unless there's appropriate planning, the worst-case situation will happen: The government will take more than 50 percent of your estate, if you're wealthy." So addressing estate-planning issues is a critical matter. For example:

◆ Does the estate have sufficient liquid assets to pay off inheritance taxes?

◆ Have the estate taxes been minimized?

◆ Should your parents give away assets as gifts before they die?

◆ Have they made contingency plans for possible incompetency?

◆ Should they create a trust or a family limited partnership? If so, what kind?

◆ Have they chosen a good estates lawyer, executor, or trustee?

◆ Have they taken full advantage of inheritance-tax exemptions and life-insurance vehicles?

◆ Have their assets been titled appropriately?

◆ Are current, appropriate wills, trusts, living wills, and durable powers of attorney in place?

◆ Does the will reflect the laws in their current state of residence?

◆ Do they own out-of-state property? (If so, different laws may apply to that property.)

◆ Have they made funeral arrangements or specified their wishes?

If you take the proper steps early—say, by boning up on estate issues, urging your living parents to write a will, and helping them to draft it—you'll play a role in these decisions, save tax dollars, and experience the rewarding feeling of exercising control over your destiny. But if you and your parents shut your eyes to the inevitability of death, these critical decisions will most likely be made for you by strangers while you stand helplessly aside.

Since today's "baby boomers" tend to be more financially astute than their parents, your aging parents may
be grateful for your help. But technically, even 60-year-
old "children" have no birthright to their parents'
assets. In every state except Louisiana, your parents may
totally disinherit you if they so desire—and, what's
more, they're not even obligated to tell you they're
doing it. The law grants you little or no right even to
information about your parents' finances.

But legal rights are usually beside the point when
you're dealing with your parents. However much your
parents may sometimes frustrate you, they're not your
adversaries; most likely, they want what's best for you.
In that case, you need psychological and communications skills more than legal rights. So persuasion—not
litigation—is the key.

(If your parents are your adversaries and you've
stopped communicating with them, you do need a
lawyer—in which case, skip to *Part 2, Choosing Professional Advisers, page 102.*)

"Ninety percent of the problems in inheritance can
be avoided by talking to your parents before they die,"
says John Levy, a Mill Valley, California, psychologist
who specializes in the problems of inheritors. But, of
course, that's easier said than done. Levy says he constantly encounters situations where "parents go to considerable expense, trouble, and discomfort to conceal
the magnitude of their fortunes" from their children.
And even the most sensitive and communicative parents and children get dry in the throat when it comes
to discussing death or money with each other. More
than half the people who responded to a 1997 financial survey said they never discuss finances with their
parents, and most of them professed little understanding of what their parents would want done with
their money or health care should their elders become
unable to make their own decisions.

"Talking about finances is more difficult than talking about sex," says David Diesslin, a financial planner in Fort Worth, Texas.

But it's also vital. "Most parents want to help their kids but don't know how unless you give them some clues," says Michael Harris, a Philadelphia, Pennsylvania, estates lawyer. "Maybe you don't need money and would prefer that your parents pass it on directly to your children. Or maybe you don't want your parents giving money directly to your kids. Either way, you must communicate your wishes to your parents."

I know what you're thinking: "It's my parents' money, not mine. So it's none of my business." But one day it will be your money, and your business. And your future happiness is important not only to you, your spouse, and your children, but to your parents as well. So you need to be as savvy about your inheritance from your end as your parents need to be from theirs.

They need a strategy for preserving and enhancing your material inheritance, and so do you—not because you and your parents are adversaries, but because your mutual happiness depends on understanding each other's perspectives. In the process of developing a strategy, you may learn more about yourself and your relatives, and you may enrich your relationships with your parents or your spouse, in the best sense of the term "enrich."

OPENING THE CONVERSATION

BEFORE YOU TALK TO YOUR PARENTS, FIRST TALK TO YOURSELF

◆ **Ask yourself: "What's my basic goal here?"** Your ultimate goal is not money but happiness, which money can't buy. If your basic goal is simply to get the most money for yourself—without regard for your parents, siblings, or others—any strategy you employ will ultimately backfire. As the aphorist Frank Tyger once observed, "If you want happiness, provide it to others." Your basic goal is to assure the fairest result for

A CHECKLIST OF EMOTIONAL INHERITANCE ISSUES

A LITTLE SELF-KNOWLEDGE can go a long way. Before you talk to your parents about their desires regarding inheritance, suggests author and lawyer Gerald Le Van of Charlotte, North Carolina, ask yourself these questions:

◆ Do you as an heir seem prepared to manage wealth and to handle its responsibilities?

◆ Are there taboos or understandings in your family that certain questions should not be asked or certain information not divulged? If so, why? Does your family give reasons for forbidding discussion of the family's assets? Have these reasons been communicated and discussed adequately? Are you sure?

◆ Are you aware of any unresolved conflicts or suspicions (possibly unexpressed) among family members? Would you really know if such conflicts or suspicions existed? If they did exist, what would you do about them?

you, your parents, and your siblings.

◆ **Ask yourself: "Whose money Is It, anyway?"** recommends Fort Worth, Texas, financial planner David Diesslin. "That creates the necessary humility. And remind yourself that you want what's best for your parents. The direct approach can cause a lot of heartfelt anxiety. Subtlety is the preferable way."

◆ **Then ask yourself, "How do my parents perceive me?"** Remember: Your parents first met you as a helpless baby. They may still see you that way, even if this perception is utterly invalid. You need to gain their confidence so they realize that you're no longer a seven-year-old, but a stable adult. Some parents, for whatever complex psychological reasons, may simply refuse to acknowledge that you've grown up. In that case, you may have difficulty ever engaging them in detailed discussions of estate issues. But at least you may be able to help nudge them in the direction of advisers with whom they (and you) feel comfortable.

◆ **Next, ask yourself: "What do my parents want?"** Your primary concern may be the distribution of your parents' estate. But that's only one of their concerns, which probably include:

— Preserving their dignity and sense of control.
— Providing care for themselves should they no longer be able to handle their day-to-day needs.
— Assuring security in their old age and for the surviving spouse. (Most Americans plan to leave everything to their spouses.)
— Avoidance of family conflict.
— Access to legal documents, financial statements, contacts, and instructions.
— Appointing an appropriate executor.
— Funeral arrangements.
— Preservation of the family business.

"It is very important that the parents continue to feel that they are making the decisions, maintaining self-esteem," says Martha Kapouch, a financial planner in West Hartford, Connecticut. "The best thing you can do for yourself and your parents is to encourage them to continue to exercise their minds and bodies to the fullest."

And probably one big question on your parents' minds is: How much should they tell you about your inheritance? They're afraid they'll stifle your initiative if they promise you a big inheritance; but they also worry about causing you anxiety if you're uncertain about what you'll receive when they're gone. This dilemma explains why many parents put off discussing inheritance issues with their children. Addressing your parents' concerns (rather than your own) will allay their fears that you're greedy, and it will demonstrate your maturity. That should make them more comfortable about discussing these matters with you (see sample scenarios on *page 23*).

◆ **Finally, ask yourself, "What cards do I hold in these discussions?"** As your parents grow older and frailer, they will increasingly depend on you and your siblings. And after they die, they will be entirely dependent on you and others (such as their lawyer and accountant) to transmit their wishes to posterity. In short, they need you as much as you need them—and the knowledge of this mutual dependence between generations can make them receptive to arrangements they wouldn't have considered when they were younger, and you were just growing up. For example:

In 1968, at age 87, retired stockbroker William Longstreth gave his Main Line Philadelphia mansion to his son Thacher in exchange for Thacher's pledge to support him for the rest of his life. After William died six years later, Thacher sold the mansion for close to $500,000. This was a good deal for father and son alike: The father got lifetime security, and the son got a valuable property. (In the absence of such an agreement, Thacher probably would have inherited the mansion jointly with his two siblings, and William would have lacked the support that he negotiated with Thacher.)

In the 1980s, a small-town Indiana banker, the third generation of his family to own the bank, wanted assurance that the bank would remain in the family after he died. But his three sons had all migrated to more exotic locales and had little desire to return to their small-town roots. They agreed to return and work in the bank if their father turned over his bank stock to them at that point, rather than waiting until he died. The father acquiesced. As things turned out, this wasn't such a good deal for the father: The sons subsequently sold the bank out of the family. But this example illustrates the leverage that children can exercise with their parents.

AFTER TALKING TO YOURSELF, CONFER WITH YOUR SIBLINGS

To gain your parents' confidence, you need a united front. If you approach your parents alone, "you'll be ostracized" by your siblings, says Katherine Gibson of the Inheritance Project, a support service, who has traveled this road herself (see *Part 2, page 116*). "You need to line up allies and develop strategies." What's more, if you help your parents plan their estate without input from your siblings, your siblings might subsequently contest your parents' wills on the grounds that you exerted "undue influence" on them. (For more on contested wills, see *page 46*, and *Part 2, page 95*.)

To confer with your siblings, choose a normal family gathering, such as a birthday or a holiday, for a conference. When you get together, sort out the hot-button emotional items. Maybe you'll find that you want the vacation house, your sister wants the grand piano, and your brother wants the art collection—and these things mean more to each of you than a strictly even distribution of assets. With this knowledge, you'll be able to approach your parents on behalf of your siblings rather than yourself. Again, if your parents perceive that you're thinking about their needs or your siblings' needs, they're more likely to think kindly about what they should do for you.

Within any family, some children are more capable and responsible than others. Parents tend to treat these children differently, as they probably should. If your parents perceive you (rightly or wrongly) as immature or irresponsible, that's one more reason to confer first with your siblings. Maybe a brother or sister is better suited to approach your parents than you are. (See the sidebar, "Fairness—Not Equity—for Siblings," *pages 24–25*.)

BEFORE APPROACHING YOUR PARENTS,
YOU MAY WANT TO CONSULT A PROFESSIONAL
Sooner or later you'll need help from financial planners, lawyers, and even psychologists. In some cases—
especially where the lines of communication among
relatives are weak—these experts can help you before
you talk to your parents. A financial planner, for example, can identify the issues your parents need to confront. Or a family therapist can help you and your siblings figure out which parent to approach first, and
which sibling should do the approaching. (For tips on
choosing financial planners, lawyers, and psychologists, see *Part 2, page 102.*)

APPROACHING YOUR PARENTS
"It's rarely the younger generation who open the lines
of communication about wills and estates," says
Philadelphia estate lawyer Norman E. Donoghue II.
"They look grabby if they do."

But if your parents won't open the discussion, then
the ball is in your court. In that case, remember:
Patience is critical. This process will work only if your
parents want your help. Forcing your help on them is
counterproductive. "You can really turn a parent off,"
says Donoghue. "They want to think they're in control.
A lot depends on where the child is in his or her life."

So if you do approach your parents, do so very cau-
tiously. And give the process time.

◆ **Here are some suggested scenarios from experts:**

**IF YOU HAVE CHILDREN OF YOUR OWN—OR EVEN IF YOU
DON'T—DRAW UP YOUR OWN WILL,** and seek your parents' advice on how to go about doing it. It's a good
way to open the subject with them. "By talking about
issues they might not have considered, you can educate them," says planner Martha Kapouch. (For a
discussion of technical estate-planning issues, see
Part 1, page 33.)

WORK UP YOUR OWN FINANCIAL PLAN—say, a summary of your major assets and liabilities—and share it with your parents. This gives them insight into your financial condition; more important, it opens the dialogue.

FAIRNESS—NOT EQUITY—FOR SIBLINGS

THE *WASHINGTON POST* STORY

BEFORE APPROACHING your parents, you need to appreciate not only what they want, but also what your siblings want. Most psychologists, estate lawyers, and financial planners point out that siblings really want fairness—not necessarily equal treatment—from their parents. If, say, one child is running the family business while the others show no interest in the enterprise, it's unfair to ask the parents to split the business equally among all their children. Eugene Meyer's transfer of the *Washington Post* in 1948 is a case in point.

Meyer was a 58-year-old financier with five children when he bought the *Post* at a bankruptcy auction in 1933. Among his children, only his daughter Katharine, then 16, showed interest in the paper. She subsequently worked there sporadically and often advised her father. But since she was a woman, she wasn't seriously considered as his successor. Her husband, Philip Graham, became the *Post*'s associate publisher in 1946. The following year, the Meyers gave Philip and Katharine a gift of 350 of their 5,000 Class A shares—the company's only voting shares.

And in mid 1948 Eugene Meyer, then 73, decided to pass control of the *Post* on to the Grahams. To effect this transfer, Meyer and his wife Agnes gave the Grahams a $75,000 gift to help them buy 4,650 more Class A shares in the *Post* at $48 per share, to bring the Grahams' total stake to 100 percent of the company's 5,000 voting shares. Two years later, the Meyers gave the rest of their *Post* shares to the family foundation, effectively assuring that the family—specifically, the Grahams—would remain in control.

ASK YOUR PARENTS ABOUT THEIR CONCERNS. Are they worried about outliving their money? Do they have health care anxieties? Are they concerned about either living alone or in a nursing home? Try to approach these questions casually. When your parents do start

This wasn't as much of a windfall for the Grahams as it might seem, since at that point the *Post* was losing money and its survival depended largely on the Grahams' own efforts. Nevertheless, such a gift to one child could have created huge resentments among Katharine Graham's four siblings. So in order to preserve a sense of fairness, Meyer gave an equal amount of money to each of Katharine's siblings at that time.

"There were a few tense moments when my father told them about the arrangements," Katharine wrote in her 1997 memoir, *Personal History,* "but nothing like the difficulties that were to develop in other newspaper families." Katharine's brother Bill decided at this point to pursue a medical career, and was subsequently given the opportunity to invest in the *Post.*

Katharine's three sisters responded very differently to identical treatment. "Flo, who was already estranged from the family, was, with some difficulty, reassured by my father that she and her children were being fairly dealt with. Bis and Ruth, who had every right to feel unevenly treated, have remained generous, loyal, loving, and supportive in every way. They were left secure but not affluent compared with my brother and myself. They were never given the opportunity to buy *Post* stock, largely because it was worth very little in the beginning and was regarded as risky." In effect, Eugene Meyer's gift of the deficit-plagued *Washington Post* to his daughter Katharine was a gift bearing dubious value and tremendous risk at the time it was made. It became valuable only because Katharine and her husband made it valuable—and her siblings, for the most part, subsequently acknowledged as much.

to talk, don't belittle their fears. You may not be able to solve the issues that trouble them, but you can listen—and that in itself will make them more receptive to discussing inheritance issues with you farther down the road.

SEEK ADVICE FROM YOUR PARENTS ABOUT YOUR HEALTH-CARE CONCERNS FOR YOURSELF. Deena Katz, of Coral Gables, Florida, asked her mother to assume a "health care power of attorney," which gave her mother the power to make health decisions if Katz were incapacitated. "From that conversation we segued into estate issues," Katz says. "We went from 'What happens if I'm incapacitated?' to 'What happens if you die?'"

IF YOU HAVE AN IMMEDIATE PRESSING FINANCIAL NEED—for capital to start a business, for instance, or tuition for graduate school—explain your need to your parents. Instead of asking them for an outright gift (which could reflect greed or irresponsibility), ask them if they could advance you the funds against your inheritance. Whether or not they acquiesce, it's a way to open the subject of your inheritance.

WHAT IF YOU MAKE A GOOD LIVING AND DON'T NEED YOUR PARENTS' ASSETS—but you don't want those assets to be lost to the government through inheritance taxes? In that case, approach your parents and suggest a generation-skipping trust that would preserve their assets for your children. Otherwise, the idea might not have occurred to them (they may know as little about your finances as you know about theirs). If the idea of skipping generations has occurred to them, they may be reluctant to do so for fear of making you feel rejected. If you suggest the idea, they'll suffer no such qualms. (For more on generation-skipping trusts, see *Part 1, page 63.*)

IF YOU'RE A BUSINESS PERSON, DOCTOR, ACCOUNTANT, LAWYER—anyone vulnerable to malpractice suits or creditors—say to your parents, "I don't know what you've provided for me, but whatever you've provided—please, put it in a trust." This tactic protects those assets from a malpractice or bankruptcy judgment. It's also an opening that could help you play a role in your parents' choice of a trustee—the administrator who controls the trust. And since you're not asking for money specifically—only that it be put in trust—this tactic isn't likely to generate resentment from your siblings. (For more on trusts, see *Part 1, page 50.*)

IF YOUR PARENTS HAVE CREATED A TRUST ALREADY, ask them to introduce you to their trust officers and their lawyers, so these advisers won't perceive you as a complete stranger after your parents die. This is good for your parents, too: It assures them of some continuity of the family's affairs after they're gone.

IF YOUR PARENTS SUSPECT YOUR MOTIVES, allay their concerns by encouraging them to talk to a financial planner. This tactic introduces an unbiased third party to the dialogue. Most financial planners will arrange a free initial consultation. (For more on choosing a financial planner, see *Part 2, page 111.*)

◆ **Here are several possible approaches to getting the conversation started with your parents, offered by experts in the field:**

"After you've worked all your life, it's a shame to let the government take so much of what you've made. Why don't you do some planning?" (Charles Plotnick, estate lawyer, Philadelphia, Pennsylvania)

"We don't care what happens to us. But what about your grandchildren?" (Plotnick)

"Hey—have you been following all this talk about changes in the tax laws? We've been looking into it—let me tell you some of the things we're doing." (Plotnick)

"Dad, is there anything I should know that will help me do good financial planning now?" (Myra Salzer, financial planner, Money Strategies Inc., Boulder, Colorado)

LAUNCHING THE DIALOGUE: TWO CASE HISTORIES

WARREN MACKENSEN: BETTER LATE THAN NEVER

"Dad, how much did you pay for this house?" 12-year-old Warren Mackensen asked his father one day.

"None of your business," replied Frank Mackensen, a Vermont innkeeper.

Warren Mackensen subsequently became a professional financial planner himself in New Hampshire—but thanks to that chance remark, more than 25 years passed before he again raised a financial issue with his parents.

After the senior Mackensens retired to California in 1982 they created a "living trust"—a vehicle that enables elderly people to manage their own assets jointly with a co-trustee, who can take charge in the event of the grantor's death or incapacity (see *pg. 42*). As trustee they appointed Warren's older sister, a travel agent who lived near them. Although Warren was presumably better qualified to advise his parents, still he declined to interfere.

An opportunity to broach the subject finally arose in 1984, when Warren's mother suffered a minor heart attack. In a heartfelt letter to his father, Warren, then 36, discussed his own estate plans, then added, "I'm really in the dark about your estate planning. I would appreciate it if Sister and I could learn what our roles are."

The effect, says Mackensen, was "as if a millstone had been lifted from my father's shoulders." On his parents' next visit to New Hampshire, they brought along all their estate planning materials—and Warren quickly found needed improvements.

For one thing, many of his parents' assets hadn't been placed in their living trust. For another, their assets had grown beyond $600,000—the level at which an individual's estate was then exempted from federal gift or death taxes (it's now increasing gradually from $625,000 to $1 million between 1998 and 2006). (See "Estate tax exemptions," *pg. 33*.)

At Warren's suggestion, his parents amended their joint living trust, stipulating that $500,000 be shifted into a "bypass trust" to be automatically created for the surviving spouse upon the death of the first spouse. In this way the parents received closer to the maximum $1.2 million estate tax exemption for a couple, instead of only $600,000. (For more on bypass trusts, see *pg. 59*.) They also amended their living trust to designate Warren and his sister as equal co-trustees.

Thanks to this planning, when Warren's mother died in 1993, the family needed only an hour in a lawyer's office to transfer the couple's joint assets to the father's successor trust. And after Frank Mackensen died the following year, the entire estate was fully distributed within six weeks. To Warren, the moral of the story is: "You have to put your childhood experiences aside."

MELISSA HAMMEL: INSPIRED BY A CEMETERY

For Melissa Hammel of Brentwood, Tennessee, the key to opening the dialogue was a family visit to a cemetery in 1994, when she was 29. As Melissa and her parents decorated their ancestors' graves, she remarked, "I need to know where you want to be buried and what your wishes are." That comment led to Melissa's first talk about inheritance with her father, financial planner Richard Hammel, then 57.

Another opportunity arose two years later. While getting a divorce, she revised her will and sent a copy to her parents. Richard Hammel responded with some common-sense observations that hadn't occurred to her. For example, Melissa's will simply divided her modest assets by percentages among some 10 friends and charities. Her father pointed out that after Melissa's parents died and she inherited their vastly greater property, such a formula would result in windfalls for a few people and organizations. In that case, he suggested, she'd want to expand the number of beneficiaries. Melissa agreed.

"You'll have a lot more control over your estate if your children know what's happening than if we don't. Why not share your intentions with us, so we know what you have in mind?" (Deena Katz, financial planner, Coral Gables, Florida)

Once the lines of communication are open, you and your parents can move on to the technical matters that need to be addressed for a smooth transfer of wealth (see the section on estate-planning issues, *page 33*). Then it's a matter of reaching agreement on fundamental issues and of hiring the right professionals to implement the details.

"The key," says Fort Worth financial planner David Diesslin, "is to know your heart—and then bring in a capable heart surgeon."

If in spite of all the above strategies and advice, your parents still refuse to discuss inheritance issues, it's time to consider alternative strategies.

Obtain a copy of "Intergenerational Accord Eases Estate Planning," an article by estates lawyer Gerald Le Van, in the December 9, 1996, issue of the *National Law Journal,* available at most public libraries. Its theme: "Children who are included in family estate planning are less likely to later challenge the will." Anonymously send your parents a copy of the article.

Enlist a lawyer, planner, or therapist to help approach your parents. But remember: You have no legal right to your parents' assets, or even (in most cases) to information about their assets. In any case, it's a good idea to line up advisers of your own now, so you have relationships in place when you need them.

If all else fails, you'll have to deal with your parents' estate arrangements after the fact. Skip ahead to Part 2, "When Wealth Changes Hands."

ASSEMBLING YOUR PARENTS' VITAL DOCUMENTS

YOU'VE SUCCESSFULLY OPENED a conversation about inheritance with your parents. Now what? A good way to start is to make sure all their vital documents are in order and accessible. Good record keeping benefits them as well as you because a will is very unlikely to document all the assets; even if it does, many items (such as life insurance proceeds, pensions, Social Security, and veterans' benefits) are often unaffected by wills and therefore unmentioned.

Here's a checklist of major documents:

◆ **The will.** It's the most important of all legal documents (see *page 43*).

◆ **Trust documents, if any.** A trust is the major estate-planning technique (see *page 50*).

◆ **Durable power of attorney.** A document appointing someone else to manage one's affairs (see *page 39*).

◆ **Advance medical directives.** Your parents can provide instructions in case they become incompetent. A **MEDICAL POWER OF ATTORNEY** can appoint a proxy to make medical decisions for them. A **LIVING WILL** instructs physicians to avoid life-saving measures in hopeless situations. Without these directives, you could face a situation in which a comatose parent is maintained on life-support systems for years, at a cost of hundreds of thousands of dollars, because no provision was made for allowing the patient to die, and no relative is willing to make that decision on her own.

◆ **Safety deposit box.** Note its location, contents, and who has a key.

◆ **Life and accident insurance.** List your parents' policies. Older people often have several small insurance policies, accumulated over the years. When you find old policies, don't throw them out until you've checked them carefully to be sure they have lapsed: They may have a cash value. Check the beneficiary status as well.

◆ **Health and long-term care insurance policies.** If your parents' health deteriorates, these can spell the difference between financial comfort and financial ruin. But they're worth very little if you don't know where to find them.

◆ **Homeowner's insurance.** Check your parents' homeowner's policy. Your parents need to be covered for at least 80 percent of the current value of their home. If they own antiques, jewelry, rugs, coins, etc., they may need a rider added to their policy.

◆ **Auto insurance.** Locate their policy and see if your parents are adequately covered. Have they taken advantage of discounts? (If they drive fewer than 7,500 miles a year, for example, they may be eligible for a discount.) They may need to increase their liability coverage.

◆ **Funeral and burial instructions.** If your parents are frail and failing, you may want to talk to them about their funeral and burial wishes. This won't be easy, of course. Keep the instructions in an accessible place. (For more on funeral arrangements, see *page 87*.)

◆ **Names and addresses of debtors.** Who owes your parents money, and how much? If these receivables are still due when they die, they should go into your parents' estate. But they're unlikely to be paid back if you don't know about them.

◆ **Names and addresses of creditors.** Your parents' debts will be charged against their estate before any assets are distributed. How much do your parents owe, and to whom? Have your parents borrowed money from a relative or friend? Has anyone filed a lawsuit against them?

◆ **Compile a list of all their advisers.** Include doctors, lawyers, accountant, minister, auto mechanic, plumber, close friends, and relatives—anyone you might need to contact if something happens to your parents.

Ideally, encourage your parents to keep these papers together in a safe place. If they prefer not to keep them together, compile a list of the documents, indicating where each is located.

NOTE: There's no harm in storing all these records on a computer, but computerization alone won't adequately protect you or your parents. The computers, systems, and disks we use today may be unusable by the time they're needed. Good old paper—filed in a box or file cabinet, preferably with a copy for the lawyers—remains your best bet.

ESTATE-PLANNING ISSUES

NOW YOU'RE READY to wade deeper into the nitty-gritty of inheritance. Here are some critical estate-planning issues to raise with your parents—or to encourage them to raise with lawyers and financial planners:

MANAGING YOUR PARENTS' AFFAIRS BEFORE THEY DIE
To help your parents figure out their plans for the rest of their lives, first perform two exercises with them:

1 **Create a cash flow statement.** How much do they have coming in and going out each month? Is anything left over for fun or savings? Are they afraid to touch their principal to supplement their income?

2 **Create a net worth statement.** This is a basic recounting of their assets and liabilities. While you're doing this, also check and see how their assets are owned.

Now you're ready to provide your parents with intelligent help about some of their key living and estate issues.

MINIMIZING ESTATE TAXES
◆ **Estate tax exemptions.** Each of your parents has a one-time $625,000 exemption from federal gift or federal estate tax (at least 37 percent and as much as 55 percent, plus state death taxes in most states), which your parent can use to benefit you or anyone else, before or after death. In the years after 1998, this

exemption increases gradually until it reaches $1 million per person in 2006. If your parents' assets exceed the exempted amount, maximizing the use of this exemption becomes a major consideration in estate planning. If your parents apportion their assets between them astutely, they can shelter up to $1.25 million from federal estate taxes—and up to $2 million by 2006.

The "bypass trust" that Warren Mackensen set up for his parents is one such example (see *page 28*).

◆ **To gift or not to gift?** In addition to their $625,000 per-person exemption (increasing to $1 million by 2006), even before they die your parents (or anybody) are each entitled to give away $10,000 per person tax-free each year to any number of persons, related or not. For example, if both your parents are living, and you are married with two children, your parents between them could give your family unit $80,000 per year free of gift tax (four recipients multiplied by $10,000 from each parent).

Here's another great way to avoid estate taxes—if your parents have the funds and are willing to give them: Your parents can also pay, free of gift tax, an unlimited amount for tuition expenses (but not room and board) at an educational institution or for the medical care of a child or any other person. (But these payments must be made directly to the institution, not by way of reimbursement to you or your children.)

THE UPSIDE: These gifts reduce your parents' taxable estate. If your parents' estate exceeds $625,000, these annual gifts can extend the exemption.

THE DOWNSIDE: Your parents lose the use of this money during their own lives. So they must have enough money of their own to feel comfortable about giving some of it away before they die. And they must trust that if they do give some of it to you, they can turn to you for help in an emergency. (For an alternative gift that keeps your parents in control, see "Family limited partnerships," *page 38*.)

CAPITALIZING ON A ROTH IRA. The Roth Independent Retirement Account (IRA), approved by Congress in 1997, can be an excellent estate-planning tool. With a traditional IRA, contributions are tax-deductible but withdrawals are taxed as regular income. With a Roth IRA, by contrast, your contributions (up to $2,000 per year) are not tax-deductible—but there's no income tax due on the withdrawals.

The estate-planning implications can be significant. IRA assets (both traditional and Roth) are considered part of an estate, which means they could be subject to estate taxes if the total estate exceeds $625,000. But the heirs who inherit a traditional IRA pay taxes again—income taxes—when they make withdrawals. Heirs who inherit a Roth IRA pay only the estate taxes, if any.

Suppose your father has $300,000 in a traditional IRA, and his tax bracket is 33 percent. If he "Roth-ifies"—that is, converts his traditional IRA to a Roth IRA—he'll have to pay $100,000 in income taxes immediately. On the other hand, that $100,000 won't be sitting in his estate when he dies, so his estate tax bill will be lower. And his heirs—presumably including you—will pay no further taxes on the IRA assets. If your parents want to increase their wealth transfer to you without making gifts, the Roth IRA is an effective alternative.

(Using a Roth IRA in combination with a trust can protect heirs from other future taxes as well. Have your parents consult a good tax and estates lawyer.)

GIVING AWAY ASSETS. Your parents can also reduce the size of their estate by giving away other assets, such as stocks or bonds. But first they should look at the capital gains tax implications. In their attempt to reduce their estate taxes, they could be saddling you with future capital gains taxes—because the recipient of an asset will eventually be taxed on any profit she makes from selling the asset.

For estate purposes, the government values property according to its current market value, sometimes called the "stepped-up" or "stepped-down" value, depending on whether the market has risen or fallen. So your key is to know the asset's basis, or original purchase price.

If your dad bought stock in World Wide Wickets five years ago for $10 a share and sells it now for $50 a share, his basis would be $10, and his profit—or capital gain—would be $40. That gain of $40 per share would be taxed at the capital gains tax rate, a maximum of 28 percent.

If your dad gives you the stock as a gift while he's still alive (which, remember, he can do tax-free, up to a fair-market value of $10,000 a year), you will assume his basis of $10 a share—and you'll pay the full capital gains tax when you sell it eventually. But if your dad leaves you the stock when he dies, your basis becomes the stock's value at the time of his death. That saves you on eventual capital gains taxes; however, since the stock is part of your dad's estate, it increases the estate tax.

Which strategy is preferable? That depends. Assuming your dad wants to maximize his gift to you, he must compare the estate tax the asset might incur if it's left in the estate against the capital gains tax it will incur if it's passed on to you while he's still alive. The maximum capital gains tax is 28 percent. Federal estate taxes can run from 37 percent to 55 percent on assets over $625,000.

Of course, if the estate is less than $625,000, it escapes federal estate taxes altogether. In that case, the "stepped-up" valuation is a win-win situation: It causes no negative consequences in terms of estate taxes, and it provides favorable consequences for the heirs in terms of capital gains taxes.

TRANSFERRING MONEY OR ASSETS TO SPOUSES. Provided you're a U.S. citizen, there's no limit to the quantity of property your spouse can transfer to you without incurring federal gift or estate tax, either during life or at death.

YOUR SPOUSE'S MINIMUM LEGAL OBLIGATION TO YOU. Unless you have a binding pre-nuptial or post-nuptial agreement that provides otherwise, you must consult your state's laws to determine the statutory rights of the surviving spouse (presumably you). In Florida, you're entitled to at least 30 percent outright of all assets passing under your late spouse's will; in New York, the spouse's statutory share, when children also survive, is one-third of a defined net estate that includes various assets passing outside the will, such as jointly owned property.

GIFTS TO CHARITY. Aside from helping worthy causes, gifts to charity can help reduce your parents' taxes in two respects. First, cash contributions to public charities are deductible for income tax purposes up to 50 percent of the donor's adjusted gross income. (That is, if your father's adjusted gross income is $100,000, and he donates $75,000 to charity, he can claim $50,000 of that—half his adjusted gross income—as a tax deduction.)

Second, charitable gifts reduce the size of your parents' estate and thus reduce the estate's vulnerability to estate taxes. For example, if your father's estate is worth about $750,000, and the federal estate tax exemption is $625,000, he could give $125,000 to his favorite charity—either now or in his will—and feel good about himself while shielding his estate from federal estate taxes. If he kept that $125,000 money in his estate, the federal estate tax would take about $40,000 of it, and your dad would have no good feeling to show for it. The obvious downside: Money donated to charity is unavailable to your dad while he lives, and it's unavailable to you after he dies.

◆ **Life insurance strategies.** A life insurance benefit paid on a policy your mother owns becomes part of her gross estate when she dies, even if you are the designated beneficiary. That means it's potentially taxable if the estate exceeds $625,000. But your mother can remove this money from her estate by transferring ownership of the policy to someone else, such as you or your dad. "Ownership" simply means having the power to change the beneficiary, the right to cancel the policy, or the right to borrow against it or to assign it to someone else. If you are the named beneficiary, and your mother is happy to keep it that way, your mother might as well transfer the policy's ownership to you. That way the benefit won't be taxed as part of her estate.

WARNING: Such a transfer must be made at least three years before your mother dies. Otherwise the benefit will be included as part of her estate. If she wants to take out a new policy for your benefit, she can avoid this three-year rule by placing the policy in an irrevocable trust. (See the section on trusts, *page 50*.)

◆ **Family limited partnerships.** Under this method for reducing estate taxes, a couple worth, say, $3 million can set up a family limited partnership in which the husband and wife are general partners and their children limited partners. The parents then utilize the $10,000 annual gift tax exclusion to transfer a $20,000 interest in the partnership to each child annually. In this manner, the parents maintain control of the funds—as they wouldn't if they gave the money outright—even if they themselves eventually account for as little as 1 percent of the partnership's assets. And because the children lack legal control of the partnership, the parents' assets in the partnership are discounted by roughly 35 percent for death tax purposes when the parents die.

DRAWBACK: This concept is difficult for most people to grasp, which may explain why relatively few people utilize it. It seems to be most popular among entrepreneurs with assets of $3 million or more, who set up the partnership just as they would set up a business. It works especially well when the assets are in real estate or marketable securities (see the sidebar, "Estate, Inheritance, and Gift Taxes," *pages 40–41*).

PROTECTING AGAINST INCOMPETENCE OR DISABILITY

In an age of longer life spans, the greatest fear for many people is no longer "What if I die?" but "What if I outlive my money?" or "What if I become disabled or incompetent?" This fear is shared by aging parents (who want to avoid ending their lives as burdens) and by their children (who want to avoid the cost and aggravation of caring for incompetent parents).

The classic nightmare scenario is that of the late comedian Groucho Marx (1890–1977). In the early 1970s, when Marx was in his 80s, he was declared incompetent by a Los Angeles court despite his objections. At the time, Marx was living with a woman named Erin Fleming, who contended that Groucho wanted her as his legal guardian. But after a bitter court battle, the court appointed a relative whom Groucho apparently detested.

How could Groucho (and your parents) have avoided this situation? Two alternatives:

1 **Durable general power of attorney.** This is a short document that your parents can sign, appointing another individual—such as you—to manage their affairs. (Durable means that it survives the signer's becoming incompetent; general means it applies to all the signer's affairs.) If Groucho Marx had signed such a document when he was still competent, his affairs would subsequently have been managed by the person he chose (Erin Fleming) instead of by a court-appointed relative.

Or your parents can sign a more limited durable power of attorney for health care—in effect, a "health care proxy" that appoints someone to make medical decisions only. If your parents' health is precarious, it's a good idea to give copies of this proxy to their doc-

ESTATE, INHERITANCE, AND GIFT TAXES

BOTH THE FEDERAL GOVERNMENT and the states levy taxes on estates, but the federal estate tax is by far the largest— from 37 percent to 55 percent, increasing with the size of the estate—and therefore the most important consideration in most estate plans. On the other hand, the federal estate tax applies only to estates in excess of $625,000 as of 1998, and that exemption increases gradually to $1 million in 2006. (Only about 1.5 percent of all estates pay federal estate tax.)

The Internal Revenue Code defines the taxable estate as the gross estate minus allowable deductions and exclusions. The assets of the estate are used, first, to pay funeral expenses, estate administration expenses, debts or claims against the estate, and mortgages. Other commonly claimed deductions include property passed on to the surviving spouse and gifts made to charity. What remains after these expenses and deductions—the net amount—is then taxed (assuming the net amount exceeds the $625,000 federal estate tax exemption).

The amount of this net estate that exceeds $625,000—the "taxable estate"—is then subject to a federal estate tax whose effective marginal rate can be as high as 55 percent if the taxable estate exceeds $3 million.

NOTE: The 1997 Tax Reform bill also raised the exemption for qualifying family-owned businesses to $1.3 million, effective in 1998. For a small family business, the $277,000 savings in estate taxes could mean the difference between maintaining the business and having to sell it to pay the estate taxes.

How are assets valued? For estate purposes, the government values property according to its current fair-market value—sometimes called the "stepped-up" or "stepped-down" value, depending on whether the market has gone up or down (see "Giving away assets," *pg. 35*).

◆ **Gift taxes.** There is no gift tax between spouses if both are U.S. citizens. And anyone can give $10,000 per year to an unlimited number of individuals, free of the gift tax.

Although federal gift tax rates are the same as federal estate tax rates, wealthy individuals can derive some advantage by making large gifts during their lifetimes rather than bequeathing the gifts at death. That's because the federal gift tax is "exclusive" (in calculating the tax to be paid, the tax itself is deducted from the total amount of the gift), whereas the federal estate tax is "inclusive" (the full amount of the gift is taxed). Because of that difference, if your father gives away most of his assets while he's alive, rather than after he dies, the effect could be to reduce the gift or estate tax from 55 percent to as little as 37 percent.

◆ **State taxes.** Some states impose an estate tax (paid by the estate on the net estate left by the decedent); others impose an inheritance tax on the amount each heir inherits. But no state charges both. Estate taxes are based solely on the size of the net estate. Inheritance taxes are usually based both on the amount inherited and the heir's relationship to the deceased: Usually, spouses, children, and grandchildren are taxed at a lower rate than other beneficiaries. Typically, an inheriting spouse might be taxed only 1 percent or 2 percent of the amount inherited, while an unrelated friend might pay as much as 20 percent. In some states, spouses and children are exempt from inheritance taxes up to certain dollar amounts.

◆ **The credit estate tax.** Every state provides a credit estate tax, which effectively amounts to a federal tax rebate. If the estate exceeds $625,000 and consequently is subject to federal estate tax, the state death tax is credited against the federal estate taxes that the heirs would otherwise pay to the Internal Revenue Service. The net result is that the heirs usually wind up paying nothing in state death taxes.

tors, hospital, or nursing home in case of emergency. In the best of all worlds, in such a document parents tell their children when to turn off life-support equipment. One who has done so is Steve Lewis, president of Lewis & Mathews Investment Management, a personal advisory firm in Menlo Park, California. "I have strong feelings," he says. "I want the money I have worked hard for to go to my family, not to the medical community."

ADVANTAGE: Durable power of attorney is simple and inexpensive to set up.

DRAWBACK: When your parents die, their estate must go through the expense and red tape of probate—the legal process of settling an estate—which can be avoided by a second choice, a living trust.

2 **A living (or "revocable") trust.** A living trust—created by and for a living individual—is a good way to protect both your parents and yourself from legal hassles if your parents become incompetent. Essentially, it means that your parents transfer most or all of their assets into a trust, which they jointly manage with a co-trustee (like a bank, a trust company, you or other family members, or any combination). As your parents decline physically or mentally, no further legal action is necessary; the co-trustee simply assumes full management. After their death, the co-trustee can close the trust and distribute the assets immediately or at a time specified in the trust agreement—for example, when the beneficiaries reach a certain age. (Most irrevocable trusts begin as living trusts and then automatically convert to irrevocable trusts at the death of the trust's creator—because the one person who could revoke the trust is now deceased.)

ADVANTAGES: This arrangement provides a smooth and painless transition. It assures privacy (a trust document, unlike a will, isn't subject to public scrutiny). Although it does not entirely eliminate the need to write a will, it enables the trustees to carry out their duties more quickly with less supervision and formality than executors of a will. Your parents can provide as much or as little guidance for the trustee as they wish—but once they become incompetent or die, the trustee is bound to follow those instructions just as if they were detailed in a will. Finally, assets in the trust avoid some of the cost and red tape of probate after death: Because the assets are already in a trust, they do not pass through probate, and this reduces costs and consumes less time.

DRAWBACKS: A living trust involves legal and administrative expenses—and as long as the grantor (the trust's creator) retains control, all property in a revocable trust is taxable, just as though he owned the assets outright. Also, creditors can collect claims against a living trust even after the grantor's death. (Ordinarily, a person's debts expire within a period specified by state law, as long as the executors have notified creditors to file claims, either by mail or by advertising in a widely circulated publication.)

Your parents, having created this revocable trust, can revoke it or change the terms at any time. If your parents become totally incompetent, at that point the terms of the trust are locked in. If you're a beneficiary of the trust but you're not its trustee, that means you must go to the trustee for any payouts. In many cases, it's cheaper and more effective if your parents simply assign durable power of attorney to a son or daughter or a trusted friend.

PREPARING FOR DEATH

◆ **Have your parents written their wills?** No legal document is more important than a will, yet the mere thought of a will provokes a kind of intellectual paralysis among otherwise mature and rational adults. More than half of all Americans die without a will. Presidents Abraham Lincoln, Andrew Johnson, Ulysses Grant, and James A. Garfield died without wills. So did a chief justice of the U.S. Supreme Court: Frederick Vinson. Thomas Jarman, once widely considered the world's greatest authority on wills, neglected to write one for himself.

Even those who do write wills usually fail to spend sufficient time reviewing the document with their lawyer and relating it to their specific family situation. And sometimes, after going to the trouble of preparing a proper will, they put off signing it until it's too late.

Why does a will provoke such irrational behavior? The reason is obvious: Writing a will involves contemplating death for ourselves or our loved ones—a painful process. A will forces us to quantify the relationship between people we love and the property we or they own. And from the moment of death a will is permanent; it can't be changed.

That's a heavy burden—so heavy that many people put off confronting it altogether. If your parents die *intestate*—that is, without a will—state laws will determine the estate's distribution. Intestacy laws vary from state to state, but usually one-third to one-half of the estate goes to the surviving spouse, and the rest is divided equally among the surviving children, often with a result contrary to what any thoughtful person would want. (For example, you may inherit more from your father than your mother inherits, in which case the burden of caring for her may fall on you.) In such cases, you as an heir will also incur needless legal expenses, death taxes, premiums for a fiduciary's bond, etc.

Lack of a will, even when the estate is modest, usually causes aggravation and expense to the survivors. But if you can persuade your parents to write their wills and plan for the orderly and intelligent transfer of the family's assets, you'll not only save yourself a great deal of grief; you'll also gain a competitive edge over most of the rest of the population.

Drawing up a will needn't be expensive. Several do-it-yourself books and kits are available, but even with these you're well advised to show the finished product to an attorney. According to the American Bar Association, a simple will written with an attorney should cost less than $250. More complex wills, with provisions for trusts and credit shelters, average around $750. But lawyers may charge anywhere from $25 to thousands to draw up a will. So it pays to shop for a low fee. Call two or more lawyers, explain that you want to draw up a will, and ask for a flat fee. Ask also for a preliminary visit without a consultation fee, which gives you (or your parents) the opportunity to evaluate the lawyer.

NOTE: One of the most important parts of a will costs nothing to write, doesn't require an attorney, and can be changed as often as you (or your parents) like. This is the "tangible personal property memo," which lists personal items like jewelry, books, artwork, or any other assets, and indicates who should get what. The will should contain a reference to such a list, such as, "I intend to leave a memorandum with my will concerning the disposition of certain items of tangible personal property. Such memo is not intended to be legally binding, but it is my strong wish that such suggestions be carried out."

Finally, a will invariably involves emotional as well as financial issues. For that reason, it's a good idea to consult both a lawyer and a family therapist concerning plans for a will. "Without a consultation with a therapist, a will may reflect any emotional unfinished business in a family," says SaraKay Smullens, a Philadelphia therapist. (For more on choosing a therapist, see *Part 2, page 112.*)

◆ **If your parent has a will, is it up to date?** If you know nothing about your parents' will, welcome to the club: Few parents discuss this crucial document with their children. Even if you don't get into the specifics of the will with them, at the very least ask them when they last reviewed it. Urge them to meet with their lawyer to see if its provisions need updating.

If your parents don't want to show you the will or tell you its provisions, at least try to find out where it's kept, so it will be accessible when it's needed.

NOTE: The will should be kept in a safe place, and the executor should be told where it is. But the will should not be kept in a bank safe deposit box, which is often sealed when its author dies.

◆ **Who'll be the executor?** The will usually designates an executor to administer the estate. Sometimes parents name one of their children as executor, an appointment that isn't necessarily a favor. Being the executor may entitle you to a fee (although family members often waive it), but executing your own parent's will can add a layer of legal burdens and deadlines to the grieving process. Executors sometimes must appear in court, and the process can take months or even years, depending on the size of the estate and the legal issues involved. You also undertake significant fiduciary responsibilities to the other beneficiaries, which may cause tension for you, especially with your siblings. You might think about whether you'd like to be the executor and ask your parents whom they've named. (For more on the functions of the executor, see *Part 2, page 93*.)

◆ **Have previous wills been preserved?** Even if your parents have changed their will several times, the previous wills should be preserved: If a will is successfully challenged in court (usually on grounds that the decedent was incompetent when he or she signed it), then the previous will is generally revived. Previous wills were significant, for example, in the infamous battle over the $500 million estate of J. Seward Johnson, the Johnson & Johnson pharmaceuticals heir. (See the sidebar, "War of the Wills: The Johnson Case History," *pages 48–49*.)

◆ **Plan the funeral.** Funeral and burial arrangements cost less and run more smoothly if they're arranged and paid for in advance. Funeral directors, cemeteries, and monument companies are happy to contract their services in advance because they get some or all of the money up front; in exchange, by paying now, you and your parents are protected from subsequent price increases. If you neglect to make these arrangements beforehand, you could be subjected to high-pressure sales tactics in precisely the few days after death when you're most emotionally vulnerable.

Suggested ploy: If your parents show no interest in arranging their funeral or burial, you set the example: Do it for yourself, tell your parents what you've done and how easy it was, and offer to help do the same for them.

NOTE: Since Americans move on an average of once every five years, many people hesitate to commit themselves to a funeral chapel or cemetery. But most funeral contracts are refundable or transferable in the event of a move. Cemetery plots, too, can usually be refunded or sold if you move—especially if you're leaving a populous area where cemetery space is at a premium. Check with a funeral director or cemetery.

◆ **Get to know your parents' advisers.** If your parents have a sizable estate, after they die you'll need advisers of your own. It's best to line up your players before your parents die, when your judgment isn't clouded by emotion. If you have a good relationship with your parents' lawyer, accountant, money manager, financial planner, etc., you may want to use them yourself. Even if you decide to choose other advisers, it helps to have a working relationship with your parents' advisers so you can deal easily with them after your parents' death. (For more on choosing advisers, see *Part 2, page 102.*)

◆ **What if your parent has remarried?** Studies show that most people plan to leave the bulk of their estate to their spouse. If your mother or father has remarried, you may worry about being left out in the cold. The late U.S. ambassador to France, Pamela Churchill Harriman, was sued by her stepchildren in a multimillion-dollar lawsuit over her management of the trust left by her husband, the Union Pacific Railroad heir (and one-time New York governor) Averell Harriman.

In most cases, it's in your best interest to remain on good terms with your stepparent. It's also in your best interest to assure that your stepparent is well taken care of financially. If she isn't, the burden of taking care of her may ultimately fall on you.

What to do? One solution popular with remarrying couples who have children is the *qualified terminable interest property trust* ("Q-TIP" for short). Your father, for example, can set up such a trust so that if he dies first, his second wife retains the income from the trust for her lifetime. Then, when she dies, you and your siblings will inherit the body of the trust. "This would let you have your cake and eat it, too," suggests financial planner Raj Pillai of Solon, Ohio. "It protects the interests of the stepchildren, but it also makes it possible

---

WAR OF THE WILLS: THE JOHNSON CASE HISTORY

WHEN THE JOHNSON & JOHNSON heir Seward Johnson died in 1983 at age 87, he was survived by six children from his first two marriages, as well as his third wife, Barbara ("Basia") Johnson, then 45, who had been a chambermaid in his home before marrying him in 1971.

Seward Johnson's will left most of his $500 million estate in trust to his widow for her lifetime. It left virtually no outright bequests to his children or to his private oceanographic research foundation, Harbor Branch, on the theory that he had already amply provided for them during his lifetime. The children and the foundation subsequently attacked the will, charging that Seward Johnson had been incompetent and was unduly influenced by his wife when he wrote it. If the court found this to be the case, the will would have been thrown out and the previous will revived.

During the litigation it developed that Seward Johnson had rewritten or amended his will some 30 times, in the course of which he had disinherited his children. This was consistent with the terms of his last will and so seemed to rule out the

for the stepparent to maintain good relationships with the stepchildren, because the stepparent won't be the heavy in determining how the assets are disposed of—it's up to the parent who originally set up the Q-TIP trust." (See the section on trusts, *page 50*.)

WARNING: No plan is foolproof. Financial planner Tom Batterman of Wausau, Wisconsin, tells of one case in which the father set up a Q-TIP trust, naming his second wife as income beneficiary and his children as remainders (who would inherit the principal when their stepmother died). Unfortunately, the father also named his children as trustees of the Q-TIP. Either inadvertently or deliberately, the children never dispensed any income from the trust to their incapacitated stepmother—an oversight that enlarged the principal to the children's benefit. Ultimately, the widow's daughter wound

charge that he was incompetent when he signed it. But there remained the possibility that a jury would conclude that he had been unduly influenced by his wife Basia when he gave her everything. So Basia agreed to a settlement that virtually rewrote the terms of her husband's last will.

Under the settlement, Basia received $300 million outright (as opposed to $500 million in trust, as her husband's will had provided); the six children received a total of $42 million, more than half of which was consumed by estate taxes; and the Harbor Branch Foundation received $20 million. The biggest winners in the settlement were the U.S. government—which received estate taxes of $86 million—and the children's lawyers, whose $10 million fee was paid from the estate.

The morals of this story are clear. First, if you have a family brawl over a will, the winners will most likely be the lawyers and the government. Second, it's important to preserve all prior wills. Third, the parties to a will can completely rewrite the document as part of a legal settlement, but they'll pay a stiff price for the privilege.

up suing her stepbrothers on behalf of the widow, so nobody was happy. The obvious solution, in such a case, is to make sure your parent appoints a trustee who's not an interested party to the trust.

UNDERSTANDING IRREVOCABLE TRUSTS

IS A TRUST NECESSARY?

A trust is the major estate-planning technique, and it comes in two types: **REVOCABLE TRUSTS** (such as "living" trusts) and **IRREVOCABLE TRUSTS** (such as testamentary trusts). Revocable trusts can and often do become irrevocable trusts—for example, upon the death of the creator of a living trust. (For a discussion of living trusts, see *page 42*.) This section deals in depth with irrevocable trusts.

Like a will, an irrevocable trust disposes of Dad's assets after he dies, but with one big difference: With a will, Dad's assets are distributed to his beneficiaries outright. But with an irrevocable trust, his assets are "frozen" in a trust until they're distributed years later, often to the grandchildren or to charity (known in legal parlance as *remaindermen* or *remainderpersons*). In the meantime, the income goes to a beneficiary, often the surviving spouse or children. Until the trust expires, it is administered by a trustee, who is charged with carrying out the terms of the trust. Often the trustee's greatest challenge involves honoring the conflicting interests of the beneficiaries (who want to maximize their current income from the trust) and the remaindermen, some of whom may be as yet unborn (who want to maximize the assets in the trust).

ADVANTAGES: In theory, an irrevocable trust can be the centerpiece of an effective estate plan. If the trustee is a good money manager and you're not, a trust can theoretically generate more income for you than you'd make on your own (although in practice, today anyone can obtain professional money management simply by buying shares in a mutual fund). A trust can shelter income from taxes (especially if the estate exceeds the $625,000 estate-tax exemption limit) and protect the family fortune (especially if the survivors are children, spendthrifts, or simply inexperienced at handling money). If your marriage is shaky, a trust also helps protect your assets against a divorce. In fact, many parents put their assets in trust for their children because they don't trust their sons-in-law or daughters-in-law.

DRAWBACKS: Heirs don't receive assets directly. Instead, the assets are controlled by a trustee who may not have the beneficiaries' interests at heart, or whose identity may change with the passage of time. That situation may create psychological problems for you—feelings of powerlessness, that your parents didn't trust you.

The success of a trust rests with the trustee, whose reliability can't be guaranteed any more than the reliability of any other human institution. While anyone can serve as a trustee, bank trust departments manage about one-third of the nation's roughly 3 million personal trusts because, in theory, they offer a blend of professionalism, continuity, and financial stability that your well-meaning Uncle Freddie can't match.

But in practice, beneficiaries—that is, those for whose benefit a trust was created—usually have no say in how a trust is managed. And neither does the now-deceased benefactor who created the trust, thanks to the wave of mergers that have swept the banking industry in the late 20th century. Many heirs whose parents or grandparents were sold on the personal service of a bank-managed trust now find themselves dealing not with lifelong paternal trust officers but with a revolving-door succession of bottom-line managers working their way up the corporate ladder, many of them handling 250 or more trust accounts at any given time. Therefore, many trusts can engender feelings of resentment and impotence against the trustee, if not against the dead parents who created them (see the sidebar on *pages 52–53*).

◆ **Trusts: pros and cons.** When a parent or spouse sets up a family trust, he or she usually has one purpose in mind: to make life easier and safer for the beneficiaries. Yet the existence of the trust often makes life harder, more confusing, and more worrisome for the beneficiaries. Most often, problems are caused by changes in an institutional trustee like a bank or trust company—changes the trust creator didn't anticipate and which dramatically alter the way the trust is managed.

Before you explore the variety of trust options available to your parents, you must confront the basic question: Is a trust *per se* a good idea for your family? The

PRISONER OF PAST COMMITMENTS

MARTHA GREENE BELONGS to an increasingly vocal army of trust beneficiaries who in the 1990s found themselves prisoners of commitments made in another age.

When her father, retired McGraw-Hill vice-president Judd Payne, created a trust for his descendants in 1960, he took special care to designate its trustee—or so he thought.

"He knew how money-center banks work," recalls Payne's only daughter, Martha Greene. "He wanted a small local bank where there'd be personal contact, and where I'd know the personnel."

Payne chose the Franklin County Trust Co. in the county seat town of Greenfield, Massachusetts, where both he and Martha lived. Today, 32 years after her father's death in 1966, 64-year-old Martha Greene still lives in Greenfield. But the Franklin County Trust vanished long ago into a merger with Worcester Bank Corp., which was subsequently acquired by Shawmut Bank of Boston, which in turn was swallowed up in 1995 by Fleet Financial Group of Rhode Island.

Fleet still maintains a trust officer in Greenfield, but that officer lacks decision-making authority. So Martha Greene must deal with a trust officer in Springfield, Massachusetts, an

answer usually depends on your family's situation and the size of your parents' estate. Most beneficiaries don't confront these issues until after their parents have died and the trust is in place, at which time (as Martha Greene found) it's usually too late to change. (But not impossible: see *Part 3, page 151.*) The best time for you to explore these issues is when the trust is drawn up.

◆ **Prime candidates for trusts:**

1 Heirs under age 25 who have inherited money and don't yet possess the skills to manage it.

2 Any disabled or incompetent family member.

3 Heirs who lack financial experience or time to

hour's drive away, and her trust's investment officer works in Hartford, Connecticut, a two-hour drive. A toll-free number replaced Greene's local call, and the trust's management fees jumped from $50 a year in the late 1970s to more than $500 a year in 1997.

Greene filed suit to move the trust to the local Greenfield Savings Bank, which she says is the kind of friendly local place her father had in mind (and where the management fees would be less than half those charged by Fleet). But Fleet officials pointed out that the original trust agreement made no provision for the trustee's removal. So they're fighting her suit—and charging their legal fees (more than $9,000 at this writing) to the Payne trust.

"I now have an adversarial relationship with the bank that has all my money," Greene says. "What I have with Fleet is exactly what my father tried to avoid 30 years ago." Ultimately Greene attempted to use newspaper publicity to embarrass the bank into letting her go, but to no avail. Her suit was moving toward trial as this book went to press. (For more on this and other tactics for removing trustees, see *Part 3.*)

devote to managing money, such as home-
makers, non-businesspeople, or others viewed by
parents as unlikely to possess the ability to hold
onto money or the patience and skill to manage it
successfully.

If you and/or your siblings don't fit into one of
these three categories, a trust may be more of a burden to you than a benefit. In that case, you should
probably suggest that your parents pass your inheritance to you directly. But before you launch that conversation, you must consider your parents' likely
motives for contemplating a trust.

◆ **Why parents usually set up trusts:**
   — Avoiding taxes.
   — Concerns for their children's welfare until they mature
     sufficiently.
   — Maintaining a common management for the family's
     money or for the family business.
   — Assuring that the money they leave is managed well.
   — Preventing children from making costly mistakes.
   — Protecting inheritors from the dangers in the world.
   — Protecting children from their potential creditors, mal-
     practice, or bankruptcy judgments, or from a potential
     divorce settlement.
   — Maintaining control over their children's lives.
   — Establishing and perpetuating a dynasty.

As the inherited wealth consultant John L. Levy of
Mill Valley, California, points out, some of these concerns are more valid than others—and some are most
likely not in your best interest as an heir (or, for that
matter, in your parents' best interests concerning their
hopes for posterity). If you've opened a dialogue with
your parents, you should analyze with them their reasons for creating a trust.

AVOIDING TAXES. Hardly anyone outside the Internal
Revenue Service would question the validity of this

goal. A trust is usually the primary defense weapon against federal estate taxes, which can take up to 55 percent of an estate's taxable assets. But if either parent's estate is less than the $625,000 estate tax exclusion (or less than $1 million by 2006), little or no taxes will be saved by creating a trust.

PROVIDING FOR CHILDREN UNTIL THEY ARE ADEQUATELY MATURE. This is a laudable motive in theory but one that often backfires in practice. When parents set up a trust for the benefit of their children, their implicit message to the children is: "We don't trust you." Treating young people as immature often serves as a self-fulfilling prophecy: They don't grow up, and they spend their lives as resentful children. As Levy points out, the indirect beneficiaries of trust arrangements are often psychotherapists.

MAINTAINING A COMMON MANAGEMENT FOR THE FAMILY'S MONEY OR FOR THE FAMILY BUSINESS. A good idea in theory, but not necessarily in practice. (See the examples of the McCormick-Patterson Trust, *pages 58–59*, and the Hanes family, *pages 66–67*.)

ASSURING THAT THE MONEY THEY LEAVE IS MANAGED WELL. Many trustees, especially bank trustees, aren't necessarily astute money managers. (See the example of Herman Moore and his family in *Part 3, page 134*.) In this day and age, when index mutual funds can replicate the stock market averages, you don't need a trustee to match the market; any ordinary investor can do it by investing in a mutual fund that rises and falls with the stock market.

PREVENTING CHILDREN FROM MAKING COSTLY MISTAKES. Here's another goal that's well-intentioned but usually damages children more than it helps them. Risk is an essential element of life; mistakes are our best learning tools. So a parent contemplating a trust needs to reflect on which is worse: wasting some of the inheritance, or stunting a child's development as a confident adult.

PROTECTING INHERITORS FROM THE DANGERS IN THE WORLD. Rich parents know that rich inheritors are often easy marks for swindlers and opportunists. A trust can protect children from these dangers (assuming, of course, that the trustee doesn't exploit the beneficiaries himself). But again, a trust insulates a beneficiary from life's best learning tool: experience.

Dr. Levy tells of one inheritor client, a naive young man who fell in love with a prostitute and married her. The marriage lasted only a few weeks, and extricating him from it was expensive. But in retrospect, Dr. Levy wrote later, this nightmare was an important learning and maturation experience: The client subsequently remarried and made a happy home life for himself.

"Protecting him from this experience," Dr. Levy wrote, "would certainly have saved money and suffering, but in my view what he gained personally from his mistake was more than worth the cost."

PROTECTING CHILDREN FROM MALPRACTICE OR BANKRUPTCY JUDGMENTS, OR FROM A POTENTIAL DIVORCE SETTLEMENT. Having your inheritance in trust can indeed protect your assets from creditors, lawsuits, and ex-spouses. If you're a business person, doctor, accountant, or lawyer, or if your marriage is shaky, you might indeed want to suggest that your parents set up a trust for your benefit. (Your parents can create a trust that shields assets from your creditors and taxes—but you can't. Any trust you create for yourself is not protected from your own creditors, including a divorced spouse who may become your creditor.) But when parents set up trusts for these reasons without consulting their children, the bottom-line message—"We don't trust you" or "We don't trust your spouse"—is unhealthy. These issues are useful in opening a dialogue with your parents (see *page 18*). But once the conversation has begun, the critical point is that you're an adult who should make these decisions yourself.

MAINTAINING CONTROL OVER THEIR CHILDREN'S LIVES.
Parents often use rewards and punishments to influence their children's behavior. This may be appropriate when parents deal with small children, but it's inappropriate for dealing with adults. Nevertheless, some parents hold out inheritances and trusts (or the threat of disinheritance) as a means of controlling their children's behavior even after the parents are gone.

One couple, for example, set up a trust for their daughter with the proviso that the trust would expire and the money would be distributed to her when she married and had children. But the daughter was a lesbian; in effect the trust would have forced her (not to mention her husband and children) into a hopelessly unhappy situation.

ESTABLISHING AND PERPETUATING A DYNASTY. The desire to achieve immortality is a common human conceit and one that's especially prevalent among the rich. Some seek immortality by endowing hospitals and schools; others do it through trusts. The subliminal message of dynasty-building—which inevitably seeps down to the descendants—is that the creators of the trust care more about their legacy than about their individual children or grandchildren. The net result often is that the descendants rebel against the memory of the trust creator, so the trust accomplishes precisely the opposite of what its creator intended. As Dr. Levy notes, "A much more satisfactory form of immortality is healthy, well-functioning children." (See the sidebar on *pages 58–59.*)

Parents may not acknowledge motives like dynasty-building or descendant control; they may not even be consciously aware of these motives. But in the course of your discussions with your parents, if you suspect that these feelings may influence them, you might show them a copy of "Trusts vs. Trust," a nine-page article discussing the human pitfalls of trusts by

Dr. John L. Levy (842 Autumn Lane, Mill Valley, CA 94941; 415-383-3951).

If after reviewing all the objections to trusts, you and your parents still feel a trust is a good idea, it's time to move on to the uses of trusts and the do's and don'ts of setting them up.

USING TRUSTS TO REDUCE TAXES

A trust can be created for any legal purpose, including reducing taxes. Choosing and creating a trust is a com-

CASE HISTORY: THE McCORMICK-PATTERSON TRUST

JOSEPH MEDILL, PATRIARCH of the *Chicago Tribune,* died in 1899, leaving his 52.5 percent interest in the parent Tribune Company to a trust set up for his two daughters, Kate McCormick and Nellie Patterson. The two sisters died in 1932 and 1933, respectively, at which point the trust was to expire with the dispersal of their 52.5 percent interest among their descendants. Unless all of the stock could be held together—an unlikely prospect in the depths of the Great Depression—the Medill family would likely have lost majority control of the *Tribune*'s parent company.

The company's lawyer, Weymouth Kirkland (who also represented the family), solved the problem by creating a new trust in 1932, before the two aging Medill sisters died. In effect, the two sisters put all their stock into the trust and gave away all their other assets, so that when they died their estates were insolvent and none of their heirs had to pay any inheritance taxes. (This tactic was probably illegal, since gifts made in anticipation of death are subject to inheritance taxes; Kirkland and his partners subsequently skirted this point by falsely testifying that Kate McCormick and Nellie Patterson were both in robust health when they died.) This "McCormick-Patterson Trust" was to be administered by Joseph Medill's three surviving grandchildren and could not be broken until 20 years after the last grandchild died—1975, as things turned out. Thus the

plicated matter that amateurs should avoid
your parents need a professional adviser, like
a financial planner, to figure out precisely wl
trust best suits your situation, and how to imp
(For more on choosing advisers, see *Part 2, page 102*.)

The following examples are offered merely to
enable you to suggest some of the possibilities available
to your parents under existing tax laws.

◆ **Spousal trust options.** A **BYPASS TRUST** enables a surviving spouse to avoid estate taxes on $625,000 in her

McCormick-Patterson Trust extended the family's control of
the Tribune Company for 43 years.

This legal maneuver was widely admired at its inception for
keeping a valuable business intact. But in retrospect the trust's
primary beneficiaries were the lawyers who created it. After
the death of the last Medill grandchild—*Tribune* publisher
Robert McCormick, in 1955—the *Tribune* and its sister paper,
the *New York Daily News*, drifted into management by care-
taker executives, and the *Tribune* lost ground to its rival paper,
the upstart *Sun-Times*. The beneficiaries of the McCormick-
Patterson Trust—many of them accomplished figures like
Newsday founder Alicia Guggenheim, writer Alice Arlen, and
journalists James Patterson and Joseph Albright—were
denied both a voice in the company's management and the
opportunity to cash in their shares. Only Weymouth Kirkland's old law firm, Kirkland & Ellis, flourished—leveraging
its media and political connections to grow into Chicago's
largest firm.

By sheltering the company from the discipline of the
marketplace, the McCormick-Patterson Trust didn't do the
company or its beneficiaries much of a favor. The expiration of
the trust in 1975 and the subsequent public sale of Tribune
Company stock was a liberating moment for the family members and the company's newspapers alike.

late husband's estate. Here's how it works: Suppose your father has assets worth $1.5 million. In his will he leaves $900,000 to your mother—a bequest that escapes death taxes because gifts between spouses are tax-exempt. With the remaining $600,000, your father's will creates a trust that will generate income for your mother. Because $625,000 of your father's estate is exempt from federal estate taxes, the $600,000 in the trust avoids estate tax also. Then when your mother dies, the $600,000 in the trust escapes estate taxes again—because she never controlled the trust, so it's not part of her estate. In this way, the $600,000 in the trust "bypasses" a second tax bite and is distributed directly to the trust's beneficiaries.

The **QUALIFIED TERMINABLE INTEREST PROPERTY TRUST** ("Q-TIP") is popular with remarrying couples. A rich wife, for example, can set up such a trust so that if she dies first, her husband retains the income from the trust for his lifetime. Then, when he dies, her children (perhaps from a previous marriage) will inherit the body of the trust. Thus she can provide liberally for her husband without letting him control the disposition of the assets at his subsequent death (see *page 48*).

◆ **Other trust options.** An **IRREVOCABLE LIFE INSURANCE TRUST** can shelter life insurance proceeds from estate taxes. A parent transfers ownership of his life insurance policy to an irrevocable trust for his children. When he dies—assuming at least three years have passed since the trust was created—the children receive the insurance money and the proceeds are exempt from estate taxes, because the father didn't "own" the policy within three years of his death. (If a large estate is involved, this strategy can provide millions to pay off estate taxes, so it might be worth considering even if the insurance premiums cost tens of thousands.)

DRAWBACK: Once your father gives up "ownership" of his policy, he loses the right to change the policy's beneficiary, borrow against the cash value, etc. Also, such a trust must be carefully drafted to account for contingencies like divorce.

Under a **QUALIFIED PERSONAL RESIDENCE TRUST** (QPRT), the grantor puts her house in trust for a specified period, retaining the right to live in it. After the trust expires, the trust transfers ownership of the house to a family member. When the grantor dies, the home escapes estate taxes because she has already given it away. She does pay a gift tax at the time she puts the house in trust—but because the new owner must wait until the trust expires to claim his property, the IRS discounts the value of the house for gift tax purposes (on the theory that the gift of a $100,000 house that you can't use for 10 years is less valuable than a gift of $100,000 outright.) The discount depends on the old owner's life expectancy, the current interest rate, and the number of years duration of the trust. When the heirs ultimately sell the house, they will pay a capital gains tax —but that will likely be much lower than the estate tax would have been.

For example: Bernard and Sylvia bought a Manhattan townhouse for $125,000 in 1968, when Bernard was 52. Thirty years later, Bernard found himself an 82-year-old widower living alone in a house now worth $3 million—raising the prospect that his two sons might be wiped out by estate taxes when he died. Bernard solved the problem by setting up a seven-year Qualified Personal Residence Trust and naming his two sons as trustees. The gift tax he paid was assessed on only 30 percent of the house's value, but it relieves his sons of a far greater tax burden. (If Bernard dies before the trust expires, the house will be included in his estate and the remaining 70 percent of the house's value will be subject to estate taxes. But, in any case, Bernard and his sons will be no worse off, except for the legal costs of creating the trust.)

Of course the QPRT works only in certain situations. It's best suited for cases where the house (usually a vacation home) is likely to be kept for a long time. In one instance, a Philadelphia accountant set up a QPRT for an 87-year-old man with an estate worth $2.6 million, including a house worth $600,000. The trust calls for the house to go to his daughter after two years. The IRS discounting formula gives the house a value of only $400,000. Since the father is in the 50 percent bracket for estate taxes, the $200,000 discount reduces his estate tax bill by $100,000. On the other hand, when the daughter receives her father's house as a gift—not an inheritance—she assumes his cost basis for capital gains purposes. If he bought the house at $100,000 and she sold it at $600,000, she'd owe capital gains tax on the $500,000 profit—a tax of $140,000 (at the 28 percent rate), which would wipe out the $100,000 estate tax saving. But if the father's cost basis was $400,000 and his daughter sold it at $600,000, her capital gains tax would be only $56,000—so the QPRT arrangement would bring her a net savings of $44,000.

WARNING: For a QPRT to work, the donor must outlive the duration of the trust; otherwise the house remains in his estate. In effect, this means that when the trust expires, the donor either has to move out or pay rent at the market rate; otherwise the IRS will contend that the donor still owns the house. But if the donor is your mother, and her primary purpose is to reduce her estate for your ultimate benefit, she probably won't mind paying rent to you.

Under a CREDIT SHELTER TRUST, the donor puts $625,000 in trust and, while he's alive, pays no tax on it or on the appreciation. In effect, the donor uses his $625,000 federal gift tax exemption during his lifetime to avoid paying tax on the increased value of his principal until he dies. Then when he dies, this appreciated principal—the original $625,000 plus interest—escapes estate taxes because the donor had already given it away to the trust.

Under a **CHARITABLE REMAINDER TRUST**, the donor places certain assets (usually stocks or real estate) in trust for the benefit of a charity. In exchange, she gets an immediate tax deduction and the right to draw a percentage of the original value as an annuity. The assets transferred to the trust can be sold and reinvested without triggering any capital gains tax. And when the trust expires (usually when the donor dies), the charity receives whatever is left in the trust.

THE DOWNSIDE: In effect, your parent's money has been given away; ultimately it will go to charity rather than to you. But if your parents are charitable and their happiness matters to you, this is an avenue worth exploring.

With a **GENERATION-SKIPPING TRUST**, if your parents' estate vastly exceeds the $625,000 federal estate tax exemption, they can "skip" a generation's worth of federal estate taxes by setting up a trust that pays income to their children (you, for example) for life and, after you die, distributes the assets to your children. Because you and your siblings never own the assets your parents placed in this trust, these assets won't be included in your estate when you die. The 1986 federal Tax Reform bill effectively limits generation-skipping trusts to $1 million; amounts in the trust above $1 million are subject to a "generation-skipping transfer tax" that wipes out the advantages of the trust.

So the basic questions when considering a generation-skipping trust are: Do your parents want to bequeath up to $1 million to their grandchildren? Can you and your siblings get along without that $1 million, as long as you receive the income from that $1 million? If the answers to both questions are "yes," you might encourage your parents to look into this type of trust.

NOTE: Since generation-skipping trusts last at least one generation, expert advice is vital when setting them up. (See the sidebar, "How Long Can A Trust Last?" on page 64.)

HOW LONG CAN A TRUST LAST?

IN MOST STATES, the duration of a private trust (but not a charitable trust) is limited by what's called the "rule against perpetuities." Most states enforce the common-law rule against perpetuities, which states that a trust can't last longer than the life of a named person already alive at the time the trust is created, plus an additional 21 years. If, for example, a one-year-old baby were named as a trust beneficiary, and the baby lived to the age of 80, the trust could conceivably exist for a century (79 years from the trust's creation to the child's death, plus 21 years). But that's the outside limit. If the trust lasts longer than the legal limit and the beneficiaries still haven't received all of the trust's property, the trust is considered illegal or void. Consult a lawyer for the limits within your state.

THE ALTERNATIVE TO A TRUST

For your parents, the only alternative to a trust is to pass the money on directly. In this case, they need to write a will (see *page 43*), choose a lawyer (see *page 66*), and appoint an executor (see *Part 2, page 93*). If your parents decide that a trust is the way to go, two critical decisions await them: choosing an appropriate trust vehicle—which involves choosing a trustworthy lawyer—and choosing a trustworthy trustee. The rest of this section deals with these technical issues involved in creating a trust. If you're knowledgeable on this subject, you can help your parents—for their benefit as well as yours.

If your parent decides not to create a trust, skip ahead to Part 2.

IF A TRUST IS NECESSARY

The best time for beneficiaries to win more power is when the trust is drawn up. Help your parents make their choices—for their benefit, yours, and that of your fellow beneficiaries.

◆ **How many trusts?** If you have a large family—or if you and your siblings have different tastes, goals, and lifestyles—a single, large family trust may cause more problems than it solves: You and your siblings will wind up constantly squabbling with each other—and with the trustee—over the objectives and performance of the trust. (See the case of the Hanes family, *page 66.*) You can encourage your parents to reduce the potential for squabbles by creating several trusts, and limiting the number of beneficiaries on any one trust to no more than one *income* beneficiary (those who receive income from a trust) or more than one or two *remainder* beneficiaries (those who receive the body of a trust after it expires).

Another way your parents can eliminate possible conflicts over investment objectives—for example, whether the trust assets should be invested for maximum immediate income or maximum long-term growth—is to avoid the conventional "income trust" approach (in which the trust's income goes to one beneficiary and the remaining principal goes to another) in favor of a "total return" concept (sometimes called a "unitrust" model). Under this approach, the trustee invests the assets for maximum long-term growth—and then the income is distributed each year to beneficiaries based on a percentage of principal. Under this model, income beneficiaries and remainders alike benefit from the growth of the trust's principal—and since all beneficiaries share this common goal, the trustee isn't caught in the middle. In effect, a unitrust model distributes capital gains each year, rather than dividends or interest. This approach also enjoys tax advantages, because the tax bite on capital gains (at least at this writing) is lower than on income. Ultimately, of course, this decision isn't yours to make, but your parents'. But you can help make them aware of the alternatives from which they can choose.

◆ **Choosing an estate attorney.** A trust document is drafted by a lawyer, usually one who specializes in wills and estates. Your parents' choice of a drafting lawyer is important for two reasons: First, the document the lawyer drafts will bind the trustee for years to come. Perhaps more important, if your parents are like most trust grantors, creating a trust is a once-in-a-lifetime experience—which means they're likely to be clueless on the critical matter of choosing a trustee, who will carry out the terms of the trust for years or even decades.

In the typical scenario, says law professor Robert

THE HANES FAMILY: MUTUALLY BOUND IN MISERY

JOHN HANES SR., whose father co-founded the Hanes underwear and hosiery empire, died in 1987 at the age of 95, leaving an estate valued at $14 million, most of it in various trusts for his five children. Two sons, John Jr. and David, were named co-trustees of the trusts as well as co-executors of their father's will.

Shortly before their father died, the brothers designed an investment partnership for the five siblings. The partnership was set up to borrow money from banks against the siblings' future inheritance and use the funds to buy equity stakes in a newspaper chain and other businesses owned in whole or part by John Hanes Jr. The plan was to rapidly expand the businesses and then sell them for tidy profits that would be free of estate tax (because the investments used borrowed money, not inherited money).

But when the newspaper publishing business suffered a downturn in the late 1980s and early 1990s, the brothers instead used the family assets as security for bank loans to fund the chain's operating losses and to pay off some of the newspapers' other loans. But the newspapers never recovered, and when the banks seized family money to cover the loans in 1993, John Jr. and his newspapers filed for bankruptcy protec-

Whitman of the University of Connecticut, the grantor (also called the settlor) sits down with the drafting lawyer. The lawyer says: "Whom do you want as a trustee?" The grantor says, "I don't know." So the lawyer suggests the trustee, and the settlor says "OK."

In such a situation, many trust and estate lawyers recommend bank trustees with whom they already enjoy cozy business relationships—a practice that can serve the bank's and the lawyer's interests more than those of the client and his beneficiaries. "The trustee has the right to hire counsel," Whitman notes. "There's nothing to prevent a bank from hiring the

tion. By this time David had killed himself with a gun, the estate had lost $9 million, and the Internal Revenue Service claimed it was owed the remaining $5 million.

John Jr.'s three sisters, furious at the dissipation of their inheritance, sued their brother and his law firm, contending that they had fraudulently looted millions of dollars earmarked for all the Hanes children and used it to benefit John Jr.'s personal businesses. John Jr. testified in 1996 that his sisters knew what he was doing and approved; if a proposed $22 million sale of the newspaper chain to Gannett Co. hadn't fallen through in 1991, he argued, he would have been a family hero.

The sisters' suit was dismissed by a federal bankruptcy judge in September 1997; it was still being appealed as this book went to press. But regardless of which side was right, two points in this tragedy seem beyond dispute: First, most observers close to the family agree that the rift between John Jr. and his sisters will probably never be repaired. And second, the rift wouldn't have occurred if separate trusts had been designed for each of the siblings—and if the two brothers hadn't been given the power of trustees over their sisters' trust assets.

trust's] drafting lawyer. That's good business sense from everyone's perspective except the beneficiary's." To Whitman, the world of trusts is a never-never land where "the bank always defers to the drafting attorney, and the drafting attorney always defers to the bank. The poor settlor doesn't know what's going on, and the beneficiary is left holding the bag. If I ruled the world, no one could create a trust without first watching a cautionary movie for an hour."

In short, your parents' choice of a lawyer is more important than you think.

In choosing a drafting lawyer, the size of the firm isn't a major consideration. This is a one-shot matter; your friendly family lawyer may be less suited to this task (and maybe even more expensive) than the biggest and best law firm in town.

Your parents' top priority should be finding a law firm that offers both expertise and independent judgment—a combination that's not as easy as it sounds. Visit potential law firms and ask questions. For instance, does the firm:

— Discuss the pros and cons of individual versus corporate trustees?
— Recommend that at least one family member (preferably two) serve as co-trustee?
— Recommend a member of the same law firm as co-trustee (a bad practice)?
— Disclose its business ties with a recommended bank, and whether the bank will kick back fees to the law firm?
— Discuss the available remedies if the beneficiaries become dissatisfied? (Most trust documents today routinely include provisions for removing a corporate trustee.)

◆ **Locating a trust's "home base."** Some states are more tax-friendly to trusts than others. Some states tax trusts on net income (after the trustee's fees are deducted) rather than gross income. Some require trusts to pay taxes annually on their income; others don't tax income until it's distributed to beneficiaries. Fortunately, when it comes to locating a revocable trust (which often evolves into an irrevocable trust), your parents are not limited to the state of their residence; they can seek out the most tax-friendly state, just as corporations do for their "official" home state. States friendliest to trusts and trust beneficiaries include Alaska, Washington, Delaware, and South Dakota. Among the least friendly: Vermont, New Hampshire, Massachusetts, Connecticut, Indiana, Ohio, and Arkansas. Make sure your parents understand this before they sit down with their lawyer; the lawyer may prefer his own state because that's the law he knows.

Another consideration: If your parents choose a bank or corporate trustee, they should consider using a trustee located in a state that follows the "prudent investor" rule, which permits fiduciaries to use sophisticated portfolio strategies for hedging risks, rather than the archaic "prudent man" rule, which limits investments only to the most cautious ones, even if they fail to keep pace with inflation. As of mid-1997, 31 states and the District of Columbia had adopted the "prudent investor" rule.

NOTE: Locating a trust outside your parents' home state may be more trouble than it's worth, especially if the distance is considerable. Your family's proximity to the trust officers may be more important than tax savings and investment advantages.

CHOOSING A TRUSTEE

This is the critical decision in establishing any trust. This decision isn't yours to make, of course—but it could affect your life for years or decades, so try to give your parents some input.

A trustee is the fiduciary selected by your parents who holds the trust's property and invests it for your benefit. The trustee's term usually lasts much longer than an executor's—often for the life of the beneficiary, or until the beneficiary reaches a certain age. The trustee's duties are both financial and personal: He or she must take a personal interest in the beneficiaries' welfare, protect the assets of the trust, and carry out wishes of the decedent. Explain to your parents the importance of choosing a trustee who will look after your welfare.

A trustee bears two primary responsibilities:

1 Prudent management of the trust's assets in a way that generates income for the beneficiaries and grows capital for the remainders.

2 Accountability to state and federal scrutiny.

For this role, investment expertise is desirable but not necessary. An ordinarily intelligent person as trustee can always hire a money manager, or even invest the assets in an "index fund"—a mutual fund pegged to stay abreast of the Standard & Poor's 500 Index or some other stock market indicator. The trustee should possess at least some sophisticated appreciation of what investing is all about—that is, an ability to ask the right questions even if he doesn't know the answers. But the most important qualities of a trustee are integrity and judgment. Technical skills, experience, and the ability to get along with family members come next.

◆ **Who qualifies as a trustee?** Any adult can serve as a trustee. A husband may name his wife, for example, or a trusted business associate. Or he could name a corporate trustee such as a bank, a brokerage, or a trust company. Or he could name a combination of trustees to administer the trust jointly as co-trustees. Naming a relative as co-trustee with a corporate trustee, for instance, can set up a balance of power between trustees and beneficiaries—but only if the relative is acceptable to the other beneficiaries. If your parents are inclined to choose a bank trustee, you might suggest that they name you or a sibling as a co-trustee with the bank.

Lawyers can serve as trustees, but they may not be the best choice. A law degree, like investment expertise, isn't necessarily a guarantee of integrity, judgment, and compatibility.

◆ **Individuals versus corporate trustees: Pros and cons.** Should your parents choose a bank as trustee (as roughly one-third of all trusts do)? Or should they choose an individual or some other kind of institution, like an investment house? Let's consider the stakes for you as a potential beneficiary.

THE CASE FOR BANK TRUSTEES: If disputes are likely to arise among beneficiaries, a corporate trustee—a bank, an independent trust company, or an investment house—may be preferable to a friend or family member who may get caught in the crossfire and ultimately exacerbate the situation. Sometimes naming a bank as a trustee can ward off IRS challenges concerning control of trust assets. (If the beneficiary can be shown to control the assets, then the assets are taxable and one justification for the trust evaporates.) Also, banks are regulated under state law (federal law, too, if the trustee is a national bank) and thus are unlikely to steal the trust assets; no such regulation restrains an individual trustee who may find control of a multimillion-dollar trust too great a temptation to resist.

A bank or corporate trustee can offer administrative continuity (though not necessarily personal continuity) over the years and is more likely to adhere to the letter of the trust documents if, say, your wastrel brother asks for an emergency cash distribution so he can take a cruise to the Bahamas.

THE CASE AGAINST BANK TRUSTEES: On the other hand, banks don't pay trust officers all that well, which means banks have a hard time competing for top-flight managers. And bank trust officers usually lack incentives to perform on your behalf or to maintain close personal ties with you—unlike money managers, brokers, or your relatives. An individual trustee, like a family member, is more likely to know you and have your interests at heart. Such a person may not be a sharp money manager, but this problem, again, can be easily solved by investing in stock index mutual funds. Don't let your parents be snowed by a bank trust department promoting its investment skills. Investment skills aren't that crucial to a trustee's functions—and in any case, if you're looking for investment skills, a bank isn't the best place to find them.

The larger the trust, the more suitable a bank trustee is likely to be. In addition to the bank's management charge (usually 1.5 percent of the principal annually or thereabouts), banks may also level "sweep fees" (for investing daily cash balances), fees for writing tax letters, for collecting rents, and brokerage fees for buying and selling the securities that usually form the body, or "corpus," of the trust. Standish Smith, president of Heirs Inc., an inheritors' support group based in Villanova, Pennsylvania, suggests that banks are cost-effective trustees for trust funds of more than $10 million but are definitely too expensive for estates of less than $300,000. For amounts in between, much depends on the protections provided by the trust document (see *pages 74–81*).

Fee arrangements can be changed or reduced once the trust is in place. (See *Part 3, pages 131–57*, for strategies.) But it's much easier if a sound fundamental fee arrangement is set up when the trust is created.

If a trusted friend or relative who is also skilled at investing offers to serve as trustee without a fee and can be expected to outlive the trust, even a small trust worth only $30,000 may be practical, and worth the legal fees.

CORPORATE ALTERNATIVES TO BANKS. If you prefer the continuity of an institution, an independent corporate trustee, such as a private trust company, may be preferable. Managing trusts is a trust company's central purpose, not a peripheral one, as with a bank. Brokerage houses like Merrill Lynch and Smith Barney as well as mutual fund companies offer low-fee trust services for individuals, and they're generally better investors.

DRAWBACK: Critics say a trustee's job is too complex for novices. "A broker has no history of dealing with a beneficiary who says, 'I want some money right now to buy a new car,'" notes Joshua Rubenstein, a New York City trust and estates lawyer.

ANOTHER POSSIBILITY: FOREGO A THIRD-PARTY TRUSTEE ALTOGETHER. In most cases and most states, your parents can designate the income beneficiaries (such as you) or the beneficiaries' children (the "remaindermen," in trust parlance) as their own trustees, either immediately or once they reach a certain age. This arrangement is not feasible when there is only one beneficiary, or when the beneficiaries are minors or disabled. But it is cost effective—there are no management fees—and gives at least some beneficiaries a sense of participating in their destiny. The trust document can specify a suitable voting scheme for decisions among the trustees or beneficiaries, and a bank or brokerage house can be used to keep custody of the trust assets (under joint signature of the trustees).

Of course there's the danger that a beneficiary acting as trustee may act irresponsibly—precisely the reason your parents may want to set up a trust in the first place. But the trust document can provide appropriate safeguards. For example, it can forbid the trustee from invading the principal. Or it can specify a specific investment plan. (For more on investment instructions, see *Part 2, page 127.*) Or the trust instrument can appoint more than one beneficiary/trustee, so each can watchdog the other.

WARNING: There may be tax consequences when beneficiaries serve as their own trustees. The IRS has long maintained that when a beneficiary exercises too much control over trust assets, those assets should be included in his taxable estate, just as if he owned them directly. This situation can be avoided by stipulating IRS-approved distribution guidelines in the trust instrument; by giving trustee powers to both income and remainder beneficiaries (usually considered opposing interests by the IRS); or by making sure that any designated replacement trustee qualifies as "independent" under IRS guidelines (say, a bank, corporate trustee, or unrelated individual).

At the very least, if your parents want to designate you or a sibling to serve as trustee, they must consult a qualified trust lawyer to avoid adverse tax consequences.

IF NO INDIVIDUAL TRUSTEE IS AVAILABLE AND A CORPORATE TRUSTEE MUST BE USED. Small, out-of-town, state-chartered banks sometimes possess trust powers and are eager for the business; furthermore, they may be more flexible and less expensive than major city banks. They are the preferred choice if the investment decisions can be delegated to an investment-wise third party (maybe the beneficiaries themselves) or if the trust assets can be invested in index funds. (Small-town banks are also a good idea for another reason: In the event of a dispute between the trustee and the beneficiaries, judges from rural counties tend to be more sympathetic to beneficiaries than to banks, claims Standish Smith of Heirs Inc.)

ANTICIPATING DISPUTES AND ATTACHING STRINGS

Your parents can attach any strings they want to a trust, provided they can find a trustee willing to carry out its terms. Here are some provisions you as a potential beneficiary should push for when your parent or spouse is preparing an irrevocable trust:

◆ If a bank must serve as corporate trustee, ask your parents to include at least one family member as co-trustee, or two if you want the family to outvote the bank in the event of a dispute.

◆ Require that the trustee provide the income beneficiaries with a copy of the trust instrument; any other agreements between the trustee and the settlor or other beneficiaries; the trust's annual federal Form 1041 fiduciary tax return; and any correspondence among the trustees or between the trustees and the beneficiaries.

◆ Ask your parents to include an "unconditional removal clause" in the trust instrument to enable beneficiaries to remove an unsatisfactory trustee without going to court. Such a clause—accepted by the Internal Revenue Service since 1995—will motivate the trustee to perform better, and it will also motivate you to monitor the management of your trust. One possible gambit to propose to your parents: Ask them to appoint an individual "trust protector" or a committee consisting of several people, relatives and non-relatives. This trust protector or committee would have the power to change trustees. Or, if the removal power is given to a beneficiary, that power might not take effect until a certain time or might be exercised no more than once every five years.

◆ If there's no removal clause, limit the size of the trust. The larger the trust, the less likely a bank trustee is to resign should problems arise down the road. A bank will fight to keep a $10 million trust, no matter what the aggravation from the beneficiaries. But it may well happily step aside if the trust contains only $200,000.

◆ Any trustee should have the right to resign in favor of a successor trustee named in the agreement.

◆ The trust document should prohibit the trustee from invading the trust principal or income to reimburse himself for legal and/or accounting expenses in cases where he was at fault. This safeguard should save you the fate suffered by a Maryland beneficiary named John Upp (see the sidebar, "Paying Your Adversary's Fees," *page 76*).

◆ Suggest to your parents that they negotiate a favorable fee agreement with the trustee in advance. When Philadelphia estates lawyer Norman Donoghue II creates a trust for a client, he tells potential bank trustees, "You'll have this trust for 50 years—in return

PAYING YOUR ADVERSARY'S FEES

JOHN UPP VS. MELLON BANK

JOHN UPP, a retired Maryland contractor as well as the beneficiary of a trust created by his grandparents, agreed to serve as the named plaintiff in a 1991 class-action lawsuit contesting Mellon Bank's trust management. The suit sought to prevent Mellon Bank from imposing a special "sweep fee" for a newly introduced trust service: the daily sweeping of previously idle cash into interest-bearing instruments.

U.S. Third Circuit Court Judge Marvin Katz in Philadelphia initially imposed $75,000 in punitive damages against Mellon, concluding that the bank "charges a standard fee for managing the trust funds and then 'double dips' to charge an unreasonable sweep fee for its services." Katz concluded that the sweep fee had generated $55.6 million for Mellon in the 10 years since it was introduced in 1981; Upp himself complained that his grandmother's trust alone had been charged $4,000 in sweep fees.

Katz's ruling was later reversed on a jurisdictional technicality, and Mellon subsequently prevailed in a Pennsylvania court, which focused on a different set of figures: Although the "sweeping" practice had indeed generated $55 million for Mellon over that decade, it had produced more than $1 billion for Mellon's trust customers, including more than $100,000 for the trust set up for the plaintiff Upp.

Following this victory, Mellon Bank sought to recoup its costs (and also to deter similar suits) by counter-suing Upp for $1.25 million—the entire value of his two Mellon-managed trusts. Although the bank lost that suit, many trust agreements give the trustee the right to pay its legal costs out of the trust's principal. Had Upp lost the suit over legal expenses, he might have been forced to sell his home.

for that certainty, give me a fee discount." Usually, he says, banks are delighted to comply. They're also willing to give up "termination fees" and other hidden charges in exchange for such a long-run asset. In any case, the fee structure is a matter of negotiation between the grantor and the trustee.

◆ The trust document should permit distribution of the assets in kind (*i.e.*, actual bond or stock certificates, rather than requiring the money equivalent) at the termination of the trust. Specify a time limit for distribution. And require the trustee to document any holdback for taxes at termination.

◆ Trustees should be required to disclose—in writing—to beneficiaries any conflicts of interest, especially in terms of their referral fees, partnerships, or investments with banks, lawyers, or companies that may do business with the trust. (See the sidebar on the Roush family trusts, *pages 78–79.*)

◆ Make sure a trusted friend or relative has a copy of the trust agreement to ensure the trustee follows the stipulated rules.

◆ Make sure all the beneficiaries have a copy of the trust document, to ensure that everyone knows what the rules are.

◆ Require the trustee to agree to lend trust funds to beneficiaries under pre-specified conditions if all or most of the beneficiaries consent. For example, the trust can hold a mortgage on a beneficiary's home, with interest set at the current rate and deducted from the beneficiary's trust income. Since the interest is returned to the trust as income, the transaction is a wash. To be sure, the balance of the mortgage note becomes an asset to the trust and is subject to management fees assessed against trust principal. On the other hand, a mortgage loan is an excellent investment for the trust: Few investments would normally be available to the trust offering the same return with the same degree of security.

CONFLICTS OF INTEREST: A CASE HISTORY

GALEN ROUSH, founder of the Roadway Services, Inc. trucking empire, left his fortune to his wife Ruth, who set up four trusts for her sons and grandchildren prior to her death in 1979. National City Bank Northeast of Akron, Ohio, was named trustee of three of the four trusts, and the Akron law firm of Buckingham Doolittle & Burroughs (which had a 40-year relationship with the Roush family) was named trust adviser of all four.

The trusts consisted largely of Roadway stock, so in 1985— at the behest of either the law firm or Galen Roush's son Tom—the bank trustee moved to diversify the trusts' holdings. California real estate seemed like a good investment at the time. To find and analyze California real estate investments, National City recommended that the law firm hire W. Lyman Case & Co. of Columbus, a commercial mortgage broker and real estate management firm.

At the time, Lyman Case was a wholly owned subsidiary of National City's parent company. What's more, Lyman Case was being compensated by developers to find investors at the very moment it was being compensated by the Roush trusts to find investments. Based on a recommendation by Lyman Case president Ted Schmidt in 1986, for example, the Roush trusts sub-

◆ **Investment policies.** Trust beneficiaries often complain that the trustee isn't generating enough income. Some beneficiary activists contend that you're best off if your parents choose a general investment strategy (*i.e.,* growth, income, or a combination) before the trust is funded—one that is agreeable to the income beneficiaries and fair to the remainders. But in a constantly changing world, the key to investment success is flexibility. The trustee should be encouraged to adjust the investment strategy periodically as beneficiaries' needs and identities change and as the trust's investment picture evolves.

Still, your parents can write some safeguards into

sequently invested more than $20 million in a limited partnership headed by California developer J. W. Theimer. For landing this investment, Schmidt received a 5 percent interest in the partnership. All told, Schmidt and Lyman Case recommended investments in 16 real estate projects.

When the California real estate market subsequently crashed, the Roush trusts suffered a loss of nearly $50 million. In 1993, the brothers Tom and George Roush sued the bank and the law firm for self-dealing and for failing to obtain "skilled and independent investment advisers."

In their response, the bank, the law firm, and Lyman Case didn't deny the conflicts of interest. But they insisted that these had been disclosed to the Roushes, that the conflicts hadn't affected their judgments, and that the losses were caused solely by the decline of the real estate market that no one could have foreseen. These issues eluded judgment when the case was settled in January 1997. But at the very least, the saga of the Roadway trusts demonstrates how trustees, law firms, and other advisers can generate business for each other while they saddle their supposed clients—the trust beneficiaries—with virtually all the attendant risk.

the trust document that should improve investment performance. For example:

To keep costs down, bank trustees will likely insist that a small account be invested in one of the bank's own "pooled" funds. This isn't necessarily bad if the pooled fund is aggressively managed. Ask to see the fund's 10-year record (although past investment performance doesn't guarantee future results). But your parents should prohibit the bank from investing the trust's moneys in the bank's own mutual funds. Some banks "double dip" by charging a management fee for the mutual fund and another management fee at the trust account level.

Ask your parents to consider specifying, or at least suggesting, that the trust's assets be invested in index funds. These mutual funds—which replicate the popular stock market indexes, such as the Standard & Poor's 500—offer market performance at bargain-basement rates. If you believe the stock market as a whole will grow over the long term, an index fund is an ideal way for any size account to match the market's performance, especially when sophisticated management isn't available. Most fund managers, including banks, can't consistently beat market averages; an index fund at least guarantees that you'll keep pace with the market.

DOWNSIDE: If the market crashes, your funds crash with it. And if you hope to maximize your income—as opposed to maximizing the assets in the trust—other strategies may work better.

Many banks will refuse to accept these conditions—in some cases with good reason. A trustee is a thankless job involving heavy responsibilities to many parties, some of whom are spoiled and unrealistic, and some of whom may not even yet be born. Many trustees won't take the job, for example, without protection against legal expenses. But some banks are more flexible than others. The phrase to encourage your parents to use with potential bank trustees (or, more likely, to say to their lawyer when he asks who'll be the trustee) is: "We're looking for a *beneficiary-friendly* bank trustee."

◆ **Other provisions to assure parental peace of mind.** Parents who create testamentary trusts often worry about the effects on their children after they're gone. They're reluctant to leave you too much money all at once for fear of removing your incentive to succeed on your own. Conversely, they worry about depriving you of funds you may need for schooling, financing a business, or just plain survival. The investor Warren Buffett, one of America's richest men, spoke for many parents when he observed that when it comes to inheritance, "You want to give your children enough so that they believe they can do anything, but not so much that they will be encouraged to do nothing."

Remind your parents: A trust document, like any legal instrument, can contain as many or as few conditions as they wish. Their fears can never be completely allayed—no one can predict the future—but here are examples of trust devices that provide healthy incentives for beneficiaries.

In one trust arrangement, the child's annual earned income is matched by payments from the trust, perhaps capped at a certain amount. Thus the more you make on your own, the more you can draw from the trust.

DRAWBACK: This approach rewards windfalls like big real estate commissions, etc. It also penalizes beneficiaries who go into useful but low-paying professions, like teaching or research.

AN ALTERNATIVE: The grantor can include a clause specifying, "My primary concern is that my children's inheritance not be used to undermine their initiative," and leave the rest to the discretion of the trustee.

When your parents set up the trust, they can specify a minimum, mandatory monthly income payout (adjusted for inflation) that will guarantee you a basic standard of living.

The trust should terminate when you attain a certain age. (Most trusts expire by age 35 or 40.) You don't want to be relying on a trustee when you're 60— and your parents shouldn't want to place you in that position.

WHAT DOES A TRUST COST?

A lawyer's fee for drafting a trust document is usually comparable with the cost of drawing a sophisticated will. This can range anywhere from $1,000 to several thousand dollars, depending on the time it takes.

Trustees' fees (usually paid on an annual basis) are

negotiable, but often run in the range of 0.5 percent to 2.5 percent of the principal under management. Leading corporate fiduciaries can be flexible. Banks will negotiate, especially if the estate is larger than $2 million. Limits on trustees' fees vary from state to state.

ONCE THE TRUST DOCUMENT IS WRITTEN, THEN WHAT?

If you don't have good personal advisers of your own—like a lawyer, financial planner, or even a therapist—it's a good idea to choose them now, so you'll enjoy established relationships you can call on when you need them. (For more on choosing advisers, see *Part 2, page 102.*)

Most trusts typically begin as revocable trusts whose terms become irrevocable when the creator dies. If your parents live a long time after creating a revocable trust, review its conditions with them from time to time; its terms can be altered until they die. (If the trust is initially drafted as irrevocable, a court intervention may be necessary to change its terms.) Your situation (or theirs) may have changed, and your needs and resources may be different. Suppose, for example, they wrote their wills creating a trust when you were in your 30s with small children—but now you're 60 and your children are adults themselves. In such a case, it probably makes more sense for them to bequeath their assets to you directly. If the will and the trust document make sense, you'll experience the least trauma and discomfort on that inevitable day when you must say goodbye to your mother or father.

PART 2

When Wealth

CHANGES HANDS

N O MATTER HOW much you've prepared for it, the death of a parent or spouse is a stressful time. A guidebook like this simply can't anticipate all the emotional situations that will arise. Suffice it to say that you're at your most vulnerable at this moment—and trouble can come from just about any quarter.

Financial planner Nancy Frank of New York City tells the true story of Pamela, who was 22 when her father died in 1981. In her youthful grief, Pamela gave her mother—who was the estate's executor—power of attorney, effectively enabling her mother to act on Pamela's behalf in all matters. (Pamela apparently didn't realize that a power of attorney is revocable.) Pamela's mother proceeded to pay herself an administrative salary out of the funds that had been earmarked as the father's bequest to Pamela. As a result, Pamela came to feel that her mother had taken advantage of her youthful financial ignorance and had spent Pamela's inheritance. Pamela and her mother no longer speak to each other.

STEPS TO TAKE WHEN YOUR PARENT OR SPOUSE DIES

THE FOLLOWING suggestions can help reduce your vulnerability, but they probably won't eliminate it.

AT THE TIME OF DEATH

Basic things you or another survivor must do:

◆ Contact the funeral director or memorial society; arrange the funeral service.

◆ Determine your parent's wishes concerning the funeral, memorial service and burial or cremation.

◆ Ascertain whether your parents have already paid for their funeral (check with the funeral director) or if they had burial insurance (check with the cemetery or burial society). If your parent served in the military, he or she is entitled to free burial (with spouse) in a national cemetery. If they're buried elsewhere, as veterans they're entitled to a $300 burial benefit plus a $150 plot allowance. Call the Office of Veterans Affairs at 800-827-1000.

◆ Notify friends, relatives, and the deceased's employer.

◆ Place an obituary notice in your local newspaper; indicate whether the family prefers mourners to send flowers or donations to a favorite charity. (The funeral home will take care of these matters for you.)

◆ Arrange an after-service reception or meal for friends and relatives.

◆ Keep a list of cards, flowers, donations, and other expressions of sympathy.

AFTER THE FUNERAL

◆ **Locate the original copy of the will.** Most likely the deceased's attorney (who should be notified in any case) knows where it is. Or your parents may have put it in their safe deposit box. (If so, you may have a problem. Sometimes the safe deposit box is sealed at the time of death.) Don't try to cope with the provisions of the will before the funeral.

◆ **Find important financial papers:** the bank statements, brokerage accounts, insurance policies, family trust document, prior year tax statements, incoming bills, credit cards, etc.

◆ **Apply for appropriate benefits.** Social Security pays a one-time $255 allowance to the spouse or to minor children of the deceased who live with the deceased at time of death. In addition, a widow or widower can receive full monthly Social Security benefits at age 65 (if the decedent never drew early benefits) or at any age if she's caring for an entitled child (under 16 or disabled) of the decedent. The decedent's unmarried children up to age 18 (19 if they're still in school) are entitled to full Social Security benefits too. Divorced widows or widowers can receive full Social Security benefits if the marriage lasted at least 10 years. Check other possibilities with the Social Security Administration at 800-772-1213.

◆ **Check the decedent's pension and retirement plans.** Some plans provide dependency payments to the decedent's spouse and minor children; others provide a specified payoff to a designated beneficiary or to the decedent's estate.

◆ **Check your local Workers' Compensation office.** If your parent or spouse died as the result of a work-related accident or an occupational disease, you should be entitled to weekly payments until you remarry (if you're the spouse) or up to a certain age (if you're the child).

◆ **Notify life insurance companies and file claim forms.** Check the policies for the payment amount, the beneficiary, and the manner in which it is to be paid out— usually either in a lump sum, in monthly sums over a fixed period, or in monthly sums for the life of the beneficiary. If it's a double indemnity policy, it may pay double the face value if the death was caused by an accident. Or it may not pay out at all if the death was a suicide.

◆ **The reading or review of the will takes place after the funeral; check with the family's lawyer.** Copies can be provided to those who can't attend the meeting in person.

◆ **Obtain at least eight copies of the death certificate.** You'll need these for several matters, from selling an automobile to closing bank accounts to settling the decedent's debts.

◆ **Meet with a lawyer to begin probate proceedings**— the legal process for settling an estate. Bring the original will to this meeting.

◆ **Insist that an inventory and appraisal be taken before any personal effects are removed from the home of the deceased.** Help the executor (see *page 93*) inventory the estate's assets. An inventory and appraisal of all the estate's assets must be filed with the probate court by the executor, generally within 90 days of death. Be sure the executor or trustee ascertains all outstanding mortgages and other debts.

WARNING: Don't pay off your dead parent's credit cards or other bills from your own funds. You're not legally responsible for your parents' debts. At death, your parent is responsible for his or her debts only to the extent of his or her assets. Also, the estate taxes are levied on the net value of the estate; so if you pay off the estate's debts yourself, you increase the net value of the estate and thus also increase the taxes the estate will pay.

◆ **Notify banks.** Change the ownership of joint accounts by removing the decedent's name.

◆ **Notify stockbrokers.** Change the ownership of jointly held stocks by removing the decedent's name. Suspend any open orders the decedent may have placed.

◆ **Notify credit card companies.** Close the decedent's accounts and destroy the cards.

◆ **Contact airlines.** Frequent-flier miles can be transferred after death. If the will doesn't specify who should receive them, ask the airline to transfer them to the decedent's primary beneficiary.

◆ **Call the decedent's auto insurance company,** to make sure the car is covered until it's assigned to its next owner.

◆ **Call the decedent's property insurance agent** to make sure that the home and contents are properly insured during the estate's administration.

◆ **Check the Office of Veterans Affairs** (800-827-1000). Above and beyond burial benefits, certain benefits, including pension and tuition aid, may be available to you and other heirs if the decedent received an honorable discharge.

IN THE MONTHS AFTER DEATH

◆ **Don't expect the estate to be settled quickly.** It can take two or three years, especially if the IRS has questions about the estate tax return. But the estate's assets need not be frozen during this period; advances against bequests can be made, and so can estimated estate tax payments. Ask the executor for a timetable of the expected estate administration. Don't commit funds you haven't yet received. (See the sidebar on *page 92*.)

◆ **The executor is responsible for entering the will for probate,** but you should be aware of the filing deadlines, which vary by state. Some estates pass entirely outside of probate (if the entire estate has been placed in trust, for example). Other estates may be held up in probate court for years.

◆ **Avoid extreme changes in your lifestyle for six months to a year.** This strategy reduces the stress of mourning and prevents you from making rash commitments that you may subsequently regret.

◆ **Notify the accountant or tax preparer who will prepare the decedent's final tax returns.** The federal estate tax return must be filed within nine months after death if the estate exceeds $625,000. A state tax return may have to be filed at the same time. No federal return is required if the estate is less than $625,000.

NOTE: The $625,000 in an estate is exempted from federal estate taxes; this amount increases gradually to $1 million by the year 2006. (For more on the estate tax exemption, see *Part 1, pages 33* and *40*.)

◆ **You can *disclaim*, or formally refuse, an inheritance, usually within nine months of the death.** Don't laugh. Some people disclaim an inheritance for tax reasons: For example, a big windfall might put your estate over the $625,000 federal estate tax exemption limit, thus causing estate tax problems for your children. In some cases your disclaimer may cause the money to go directly to your children; check with your attorney. Other heirs disclaim their inheritance to avoid being bothered by the decedent's creditors—but this is an invalid excuse, since creditors have no legal claim on a debtor's heirs, only on his estate.

◆ **Contesting the will.** The deadline varies from state to state (see *page 95*).

THE ESTATE OF DONALD B.: A SAMPLE TIMETABLE

HOW LONG DOES it take to settle an estate? Here's a sample timetable for a late Florida resident named "Donald B.," distributed to clients by Philadelphia estates attorney Norman E. Donoghue II:

July 27, 1998—Date of death.

January 27, 1999—Alternate valuation date (six months after death) allowed for federal estate tax returns. (Assets still held in the estate may be valued as of this date for tax purposes if doing so will reduce the estate's taxes.)

April 15, 1999—Due date for decedent's final federal and state income tax returns.

April 27, 1999—Due date for federal estate tax return.

June 30, 1999—For tax purposes, this is the end of the estate's first fiscal year. After the preparation of tax and expense estimates and before the death, tax returns are filed and settled, and partial distributions can be made to the marital trust for Donald's wife Joanne on an estimated advance basis. The insurance trust can be funded as soon as the estate receives the insurance proceeds.

Oct. 15, 1999—Last day to file first income tax return for the estate.

April 1999 to summer 2000—Waiting for federal and state death tax audits to be completed and tax clearances issued.

Fall 2000 (or earlier if taxes are settled earlier)—Preparation of executor's final account—a list of all the estate's transactions—for approval by the beneficiaries, followed by release of the executor. Final distribution of the estate occurs upon approval of the executor's final account.

THE EXECUTOR

DUTIES OF EXECUTORS

The **EXECUTOR** is the person or institution named in the will to execute or carry out the terms of that will. (There can be more than one, but most states limit executors' fees to a maximum of three executors.) The executor is usually a family member, a professional fiduciary (like a bank or trust company), a trusted friend, a lawyer, or an accountant.

The executor offers the will for probate in the relevant court. After the will is accepted for probate, the executor:

◆ Collects and inventories the assets and debts.

◆ Gets the assets and debts appraised.

◆ Locates and notifies creditors of their need to file claims.

◆ Determines whether assets must be sold to satisfy debts.

◆ Invests the assets while the estate is being administered.

◆ Pays the death taxes (if any).

◆ Finally, distributes the assets in accordance with the will's directions. The taxes must be paid before the estate is distributed to the heirs. (In some cases, money can be distributed during the probate period. For example, a widow can ask the court for an allowance.)

This administration process can consume two to 10 years, depending on the estate's size and complexity.

Compensation of executors is fixed by statute in many jurisdictions. In New York State, for example, the executor's fee is 5 percent of the first $100,000 disposed of by the will, 4 percent of the next $200,000, 3 percent of the next $700,000, 2.5 percent of the next $4 million, and 2 percent of the balance. New York allows up to three full commissions to be paid to individual executors. California's fees are lower.

IF YOU ARE THE EXECUTOR

You may find that your deceased parent has named you the executor of his or her estate without your knowledge. If you want to decline, you may do so; usually an alternate is named in the will. If the will doesn't name an alternate, or if it doesn't name an executor at all, the probate court may appoint an administrator to administer the estate.

LOCAL ESTATE AND INHERITANCE TAXES

IN ADDITION TO the federal **ESTATE TAX** (imposed on the total net estate, before it's distributed to the heirs), almost all states in the United States impose some type of death tax—either an estate tax or an **INHERITANCE TAX** (on the amount inherited by each beneficiary). The laws usually provide that funeral expenses, valid debts, and lawful expenses of administering the estate can be deducted before calculating either tax. Some states exempt spouses and children up to certain levels, but not other beneficiaries. (See the discussion of death taxes in *Part 1, pages 40–41.*)

YOUR INHERITANCE

IF THERE IS NO WILL

If your parents left no will, welcome to the club: 60 percent of American adults die without one. An estate without a will is transferred in accordance with intestacy laws, which vary by state and generally provide for the order of inheritance among the closest living relatives. In most cases, one-third to one-half will go to the surviving spouse, with the rest divided equally among the children. If no qualified relatives are found, such an estate passes to the state treasury.

NOTE: Although life insurance is subject to estate taxes, it passes outside of probate, directly from the insurance company to the named beneficiaries. If the taxable estate is less than $625,000, of course, there are no estate taxes.

IF THERE IS A WILL

◆ **What to expect:** Your "inheritance" will be less than it seems. If the estate exceeds $625,000, federal estate taxes will take at least 37 percent of the excess (in the absence of a trust). The lawyers will customarily take close to 5 percent for settling the estate. If you're the income beneficiary of a trust, you'll avoid estate taxes, but you'll have little or no control over how the trustee will invest your family's money or the fees the bank will charge to manage the funds. (For a discussion of dealing with trustees, see *Part 3, pages 131–57.*)

◆ **Your right to access the will.** A will is a public document, available for anyone to examine. It should be on file at the office of the registrar of wills in the county seat of the locality where the decedent lived.

◆ **Contesting a will.** Suppose your father told you he was leaving everything to you. But now that he's dead, you find instead that he left everything to his new lawyer or to the live-in nurse who tended him in his last months. You can legally challenge the validity of the will during probate—but only if you can hang your hat on one of these three factors:

1 The will is invalid because the signer lacked mental capacity; or undue influence was exerted on the will-maker by family, friends, or lawyers; or fraud was committed.

2 The will is improperly signed or executed, usually because of lack of proper witnesses in accordance with state law.

3 The will has been revoked by its maker.

If a court finds the will invalid, a previous will may become the controlling document. Or if there is no valid will, the estate will be distributed according to intestacy laws—that is, as if there is no will.

Is a will contest worth the time, trouble, and expense? In almost all cases, no. Will contests are extremely costly, exacerbate family tensions, shine a public spotlight on otherwise private intra-family squabbles, and may lead to a settlement that's vastly different from the decedent's wishes. See *Part 1, page 48*, for the case of Seward Johnson's will: After he left virtually all of his estate to his second wife, his children contested the will; Johnson's widow settled after a long legal battle that cost the participants more than $100 million.

AFTER THE WILL IS SETTLED

You've finally received your inheritance. Now what? Some points to consider.

◆ **First things first.** Your inheritance may very well be the single largest financial boost you receive in your life. How much is enough to cause upheaval or disorientation in your life? That depends on the individual. If you're the family breadwinner, an inheritance—whether it's in trust or not—may mean that the family no longer needs you to provide financial support, which can diminish your self-esteem.

One writer suggests that inheritance begins to become significant if it exceeds 5 percent of your annual income. Another benchmark is 25 percent—that is, three months' salary or income. If you've inherited the equivalent of several years' salary, the inheritance will probably raise basic life issues and cause you to rethink your financial plans.

If that's your case, what better time to re-evaluate the course of your life? Set aside time to ask yourself some "dream" questions, as if your life is just starting—because, in a sense, your new life *is* just starting. A question like "If I never had to work again, what would I most love to spend my time doing?" can elicit surprising responses.

Even if your inheritance isn't huge, or even if you prefer to remain on your present course, you must ask yourself: How does this money change my life situation? What are my goals for this inheritance? Do I want to:

- — Change careers?
- — Retire early?
- — Start a new business?
- — Send my kids to private school?
- — Give more money to charity?
- — Take a less stressful job and use some of the income from investing the inheritance to make up the salary difference?

And so on. The emotional effects of a parent's death, combined with the need to attend to funeral and estate details, almost always relegates these deeper personal questions to such an extent that they're never dealt with. "That's when the money gets siphoned off into flashy expenditures or some guilt account, never to be touched," says Santa Monica, California, financial planner Brent Kessel. If you lay all your options on the table early, you can make some conscious choices that can cause a huge difference to your future life.

Once you have a clear sense of your goals, your uses of the money will fall into place. And your advisers will be better equipped to serve your needs.

◆ **Can money change you?** Probably not. the question, "Does wealth bring happiness?" has been debated for centuries. The most useful answer may have been provided by Joseph Thorndike in *The Very Rich* (1976): "Perhaps the only conclusion to draw is that great wealth may give its possessors a more than normal opportunity to become either happy or unhappy, depending on their own natures."

Depending on your nature, an inheritance can open up new opportunities or drown you in guilt. The key question, says planner Barbara Steinmetz of Burlingame, California, is: "How strong were you as a human being before you came into your inheritance?"

Studies of lottery winners invariably conclude that after a few years of big spending and high living, most of them wind up right back where they started. Inheritance is an especially perverse kind of lottery because it adds the factor of emotional loss and because you assume an implied responsibility to preserve capital for later generations.

Financial planner Nancy Frank of New York City, for example, gained a fair amount of money after her father died—but she lost her father, who was irreplaceable. She learned of her inheritance when her aunt phoned one day with the greeting, "Hello, heiress!"

"I would rather have a father," Frank replied.

Your inheritance will serve you best if you use it to build on your existing strengths. It will serve you worst if it causes you to throw over everything you've built thus far in your life.

◆ **Dealing with grief issues.** Money *per se* may not change you—but the loss of a loved one can. In the early 1970s Dr. Thomas H. Holmes, a professor of psychiatry at the University of Washington, developed a scale assigning point values to changes—good as well as bad—that affect us. In the population he studied, 80 percent of the people who exceeded 300 points on his scale within one year became seriously depressed or suffered heart attacks or other illnesses.

On Holmes' list of 31 life changes, the death of a spouse (100 points) was by far the most serious, and the death of a close family member like a parent ranked fifth (63 points). (By comparison, divorce scored 73 points, marital separation 65, jail term 63, personal injury 53, marriage 50, and being fired from a job 47.) Many other changes ranked by Holmes can be related to a death in the family: retirement (45 points), change in financial status (38), change to a different kind of work (36), trouble with in-laws (29), a spouse beginning or stopping work (26), or a change in residence (20).

The apparent lesson: Too much change within a year of a death can be hazardous to your health.

The emotional stress of death can also impede your judgment. It's important that you resolve the emotional issues of inheritance before you tackle the financial ones. Sometimes it's a matter of seeing a therapist for a few weekly sessions, or even for a year or two. Or it may simply be a matter of recognizing the syndromes of grief. The mere awareness of these syndromes may suffice to avoid the psychological traps that heirs often fall into. For example:

REGRET. You wish your dead parent had paid more attention to you and less to making money.

GUILT. You feel you've done nothing to deserve the money that your deceased parent worked so hard to accumulate.

IMMATURITY. With some heirs, a large inheritance shelters them from life's challenges, with the result that they never grow up.

LOW SELF-ESTEEM. If you come into inherited wealth before you've had a chance to make a living on your own, you may doubt your own self-worth or sense of purpose. As a result, you may abdicate the entire management of your wealth to the hands of "experts"—a dangerous idea. (See the case of Sally Lowell, *Part 3, page 122.*)

EXCESSIVELY HIGH SELF-ESTEEM. Some heirs go to the other extreme, developing an exaggerated and unwarranted notion of their own power because they are suddenly rich.

BOREDOM. Some heirs feel that a large inheritance removes the challenges from life, so nothing excites them. They fail to perceive a large inheritance as one of life's greatest challenges—which it is.

PARANOIA. Many rich people fear swindlers, golddiggers, exploiters, and kidnappers—sometimes with good reason. These fears are heightened among inheritors, who come into money suddenly and without adequate preparation, and consequently often feel powerless to deal with the family business and family retainers.

DENIAL. To avoid facing the sorrow of loss, some heirs try to handle all aspects of their inheritance as if nobody had died. This refusal to seek advice from friends or experts usually leads to financial misjudgments.

ANXIETY. Some beneficiaries are concerned (legitimately) with how they'll cope without the support of the deceased. Consequently, they try to hasten the grieving process in the hope of proving they can make it on their own. Often this haste leads to bad financial decisions.

EUPHORIA. Some heirs feel compelled to blow their entire inheritance on some "impossible dream." Huntington Hartford, the A&P heir, inherited $90 million in 1957 and promptly lost $80 million of it on a free retreat for artists, the refurbishing of a Hollywood theater, *Show* magazine, and a 700-acre Caribbean resort, none of which survived for long.

If you recognize any of these syndromes in yourself, the good news is that you're not alone and many therapists are well-equipped to deal with them. (See *page 112* for advice on choosing a therapist.)

QUICK TIPS

◆ If you've come into a windfall through the death of a loved one, resist the temptation to change your lifestyle right away, because the emotional stress of the moment may prevent you from thinking clearly. Wait at least six months—preferably a year if the deceased was your spouse. During this interim period, don't put your inheritance in anything more complicated than a money-market fund. If you blow your entire inheritance, soon you'll be back where you started. But if you maintain your current lifestyle by living within your current income, your inheritance will grow so it can fund your real needs: a house, a new career, a business, or your retirement.

◆ If your inheritance is illiquid—consisting, say, of real estate or art works—and you have bills to pay, you may need to liquidate some of your assets, which requires having the assets appraised. This is to be avoided during the vulnerable six-month to one-year period. You may well be approached by appraisal houses who, having read your parent's obit in the newspapers, promise to "help you get cash" with a high appraisal (or, conversely, promise to save on estate taxes with a low appraisal). If you must liquidate assets within a year of death, find an intermediary to choose an appraiser. A trusted relative or friend will suffice.

◆ When you receive your inheritance, suggests Nancy Frank, buy yourself a frivolous present—perhaps a new coat, a night on the town, a weekend in Paris, or something else that you've always wanted but never felt you could afford. Set a maximum dollar limit for this "present" (perhaps $1,000) or a maximum percentage of the inheritance (perhaps 1 percent). Give yourself enough to make the gift special but not so much that it will decimate the inheritance itself.

Frank, for example, traveled to Europe at age 21 as a college graduation present to herself after receiving a six-figure inheritance from a great-aunt. Nine years later, when her father died and left her a second inheritance, she purchased a pair of very expensive shoes that she couldn't otherwise have justified.

This gift to yourself accomplishes several things. First, it signifies that something special has happened to you. Second, it gives you a tangible good feeling about the loved one you've just lost. Third, it provides you with a permanent reminder that whatever else may become of your inheritance in the future, you've already derived some pleasure from it.

Most important, such a gift enables you, for a relatively small expenditure, to satisfy your frivolous inclinations. "I think it's important to allow yourself one extravagance early on, so that later down the line you're not overindulging the way that lottery winners seem to do," Frank says.

WARNING: This advice doesn't suit everyone. Some new heirs feel a tremendous burden to preserve and grow their parents' hard-earned money. If you're uncomfortable spending the money or enjoying yourself when a loved one has just died, that's fine.

◆ News of your inheritance will spread quickly— among your relatives, acquaintances, and any business or charity that reads the obituary pages. You will be approached and pressured for all sorts of money-spending ventures. Learn to say "no" or "I'll have to think about that" or "I'll have to get back to you." Sometimes it helps to have a relative or professional adviser who can act as an intermediary.

CHOOSING PROFESSIONAL ADVISERS

Do you want to tend to your estate yourself? Do you enjoy this kind of activity? Are you capable of doing it well? Or would you rather delegate the responsibility to someone else? These are questions you must ask yourself.

The larger your inheritance, the more likely you'll need professional advice—from a lawyer, an accountant, a financial planner, a money manager, a stockbroker, a therapist (no joke: see *page 112*), or any combination of these. A six-figure inheritance or greater will probably change many things in your life, and you'll need good advice for these changes. Even with a modest inheritance, you're well advised to consult the most competent attorney and accountant that you can find. Even if you only meet once or twice with them when you first receive your inheritance, their advice is critical to avoid future costs that may far outweigh what you pay now. A large estate may require several lawyers, accountants, private bankers, money managers, etc.

A basic rule of thumb, suggested by lawyers Emily

Card and Adam Miller, regarding the size of your inheritance:

MODEST INHERITANCE (UNDER $100,000): One meeting with a lawyer or accountant is necessary, assuming the executor is competent.

MODERATE ($100,000 TO $600,000): At least one meeting each with a lawyer and accountant, plus some time with an investment adviser or money manager.

MAJOR (OVER $600,000): You'll want, at minimum, a lawyer and accountant handling your affairs regularly. Consider other players as well, such as a money manager. Plan to meet once a year to fit your inheritance into your existing income, tax, and investment picture. You'll also need professional advice to revise your own estate plan.

MILLIONS: Build a professional team that you can grow with as you preserve and grow your inheritance. Work with your advisers to coordinate an overall estate, tax, and investment plan.

The Catch-22 is that the people who most need professional advisers are often the least qualified to choose advisers.

What to do? "You have to educate yourself," says New York City financial planner Nancy Frank. "That's the key to dealing with inherited money."

Choosing advisers is largely a matter of common sense—much like, say, choosing your friends.

◆ **Qualities to look for in your advisers (in descending order of priority):**

1 Honesty and integrity are the primary prerequisites.
2 Intelligence and professional competence.
3 Background and experience.
4 Comfort and chemistry. Is this someone you trust? Someone you feel you can talk to? Someone who listens when you talk and responds

sensitively? Evaluate potential advisers the way you evaluate your friends: Not every one is right for you.

5 A willingness by the adviser to put your interests first.

6 Independent judgment.

◆ **How to find advisers who possess these traits:**

1 Ask other professionals in your own field to suggest advisers.

2 Interview at least two professionals in each category you need (lawyer, accountant, financial planner, etc.). This gives you a basis of comparison.

3 Ask the adviser for references, both from clients and other professionals in his field. (A refusal, by itself, is a tip-off that you should look elsewhere.)

4 Ask to see a résumé. Ask the adviser about his education, his professional designations (for more specifics, see "A quick guide to professional advisers" on *page 107*), how many years he has practiced in his field, continuing education programs he pursues, his memberships in professional organizations. Ask about his specialties and areas of interest.

5 Ask the adviser if he's ever been cited by a professional or regulatory governing body for disciplinary reasons.

6 Ask the adviser how she will add value to your situation—that is, how you will benefit financially from using her services.

7 Ask the adviser straightforwardly whether your inheritance is too large or too small for her to deal with.

8 Ask the adviser how she'll be compensated. In most situations, a straight fee arrangement (by the hour or the project) assures you the independent judgment of your adviser. (Among

the exceptions: money managers, who generally take an annual percentage of your assets under management, and plaintiffs' lawyers, who generally take a sizable portion—usually one-third—of whatever they win for you but nothing if you lose.) For more on fee-only arrangements, see the section on financial planners, *page 111*.

◆ **Things to avoid when choosing advisers:**
1 Don't be intimidated when interviewing potential advisers. Learn how to ask questions. Remember: You're the client who'll be paying the bills. It's up to *them* to please *you*.
2 Don't use relatives or friends as professional advisers. Personal relationships muddy the ability to give detached professional advice.
3 Be careful about asking relatives to recommend their advisers. Your relatives may not want to relinquish information to you—or you may not want to relinquish information to them. Again, this depends on your comfort level with the particular relative.
4 Don't focus solely on the cost. Instead, focus on the quality and value of the advice you need.
5 Don't work with a professional who declines to hold full and open discussions on any professional matter you'd like to discuss.

◆ **Family advisers, or choose your own?** One option is to retain the professionals used by your late parent or spouse. The main advantage: There's no long learning curve; these advisers will be fully familiar with your family's affairs from Day One. The big drawback: Divided loyalties.

The advisability of this option depends on several factors, most of all trust.

TRUST. If your inheritance comes with professionals attached, remember that their loyalties may lie elsewhere, with other relatives or even with the past. Meet each one separately and ask each about matters that concern you. Ask yourself: Are you comfortable with these people? Whom would you feel comfortable calling for help at 4 A.M.? If you're not comfortable with your parents' advisers, you need to shop for others.

After her father died, financial planner Nancy Frank of New York fired the family stockbroker because she found him patronizing, and she stopped using the family's accounting firm. Why? The associate preparing her taxes giggled when Frank asked how much the tax preparation would cost. On the other hand, she still retains the law firm her family has used for 25 years "because I'm comfortable there," she says.

Some heirs feel so intimidated by their parents' advisers that they can't bring themselves to replace them. In that case you may need to hire another professional to do the job for you. One woman in the Boston area lost both her parents in her 30s and inherited their lawyer and accountant. These advisers had known her since her childhood and continued to treat her like a child. Because she found them impossible to deal with, she hired Cynthia Coddington, a Cambridge financial planner with CPA certification. Coddington was able to act as the woman's advocate and also give her an unemotional assessment of her concerns.

"When I called the accountant and he wasn't even willing to answer my questions," Coddington says, "I knew my client's concerns were valid." Coddington subsequently helped the client hire a new lawyer and accountant.

AGE. Your parents' advisers may be close to your parents' age—in which case they may not be practicing much longer. Other things being equal, you may prefer professionals roughly your own age.

PROXIMITY. Even if you see your advisers just once or twice a year, it's reassuring to know they're nearby if you need to look them in the eye. Even if you like your parents' advisers, it makes sense to replace them if they're in New York and you're in California. And they'll certainly understand if you do.

A QUICK GUIDE TO PROFESSIONAL ADVISERS

◆ **Lawyers.** Receiving an inheritance calls for two basic activities that should be discussed and handled with an attorney:

1 Reviewing the estate closing, including the will, the living trust, and the estate tax return, to insure that your parent's wishes were carried out.

2 Preparing your own will or living trust so that your new assets will be protected for you and your family.

If you already use an attorney for general personal and business advice, find out if she's familiar with estate planning. If not, ask your lawyer to refer you to a colleague who is. If you don't have an attorney, talk to friends who do. Or check with your accountant or other professionals you know.

When you shop for an attorney, interview at least two or three lawyers, in person or by phone. Take note of the responsiveness of the office. If you don't receive a prompt call-back (unless there's a good reason, like the attorney is in trial or out of town), that may mean the office is too busy to accept new business. Make sure you feel good chemistry with the professional and the staff. Remember: You're the client; the lawyer is there to serve *you.*

COST. The attorney is usually the most expensive member of your team. But remember that professional fees are negotiable, especially in an age when the supply of lawyers exceeds the demand for their services. See if your lawyer is willing to work on other than a straight-time basis. For example, your attorney may give you a flat fee for a specific task, like drawing up a

will. If he charges strictly by the hour, try to get an estimate of time and cost beforehand.

One suggestion: You can set monthly or quarterly
dollar target amounts for fees with your lawyer (or
other professionals as well), and ask the lawyer or
accountant to alert you when the fees may exceed
these pre-authorized amounts. Or you can place the
lawyer on a retainer, meaning the lawyer receives a
regular monthly or quarterly amount. This arrangement provides him with regular cash flow, and it provides you with a predictable cost level. A retainer
arrangement is best for people with continuous business needs or some other reason to use a lawyer constantly. But lawyers who'll accept retainer arrangements are increasingly rare these days.

Another alternative is value-based billing. That
means the lawyer gets more for work on a million-
dollar deal, less for work that saves a few hundred
dollars.

◆ **Accountants.** You need an accountant to keep your
books and handle your taxes—but not for business
advice. Many heirs mistakenly assume that a good
accountant is also a good business adviser; not so. If
you don't have an accountant already, find one who's
familiar with estate planning and tax issues related to
inheritance (not all accountants are). A Certified Public Accountant (CPA) is usually preferable to a book-
keeper or tax preparer, but experience and personal
chemistry should be your top criteria. Even with the
best accountant and excellent chemistry, it's a good
idea to have your accountant's recommendations
reviewed by your lawyer; the lawyer may find legal
problems that escape the accountant's notice.

WARNING: Although a good professional in any field will
keep your information confidential, there is no legal protection in an accountant-client relationship, as there is with a
lawyer. Accountants can and do turn in clients for the
rewards offered by the IRS for tax cheats. If you have ques-

tions that you think need legal protection, ask them of an attorney, not an accountant.

◆ **Investment advisers.** Investment advisers come in many shapes and sizes, often overlapping.

An **INVESTMENT COUNSELOR** is paid a fee—usually a percentage of the client's assets—to help a client determine long-run investment objectives and then find nitty-gritty ways to meet those objectives. You can usually find such firms in the Yellow Pages under "Investment Advisory Services."

A **MONEY MANAGER** or **PORTFOLIO MANAGER** has narrower goals but broader powers than an investment counselor: Usually the client simply hands the money manager a bundle of cash and tells him to reach certain objectives in whatever manner the manager sees fit. The money manager, by definition, exercises fiduciary control over the money he's given to manage— that is, he has total discretion to invest it. The size of your portfolio will determine whether you need a money manager. It's probably a good idea for a portfolio larger than $100,000, unless you're comfortable investing by yourself and have a good investment track record. Major estates in excess of $250,000 should be professionally managed—or, at least, professionally advised. Most money managers won't handle a client with less than $100,000; with many, the minimum account is $250,000 or $1 million.

Money managers and investment counselors are regulated by the Securities & Exchange Commission (SEC), where they must be listed as "Registered Investment Advisers." But this is simply a matter of paying a fee and filling out the necessary forms. Just about anyone can call himself a money manager. The SEC's regulation is inconsistent and not something you should rely on. So do your own homework.

Money managers aren't required to publish their results, so it's hard to measure their performance or honesty. But a growing number of financial planners and advisers now specialize in matching clients with money managers. Such an **INVESTMENT MANAGEMENT CONSULTANT** can also continue to monitor the money manager's performance for you. (See the section on financial planners, *page 111*.)

The money manager's fee is usually based on the size of the assets under management, usually 1 percent to 2 percent. Thus the more your funds grow, the greater his reward. These fees are negotiable—usually the more funds under management, the lower the fee percentage. When you choose a money manager, make sure his investment biases (cautious, aggressive, etc.) match your own. Fiduciary power can be easily abused, so check a manager's references directly with his clients.

A **STOCKBROKER** can be a good source of information about investing once you've decided independently what portion of your assets belong in stocks and what growth profile you need. But don't use your broker as your financial strategist; her expertise lies only in the buying and selling of stocks, bonds, options, and other securities. Among brokerage houses, you have a choice between a full-service brokerage (which offers advice and charges a premium) or a discount house (which charges about half as much but only executes trades). It's like the difference between shopping for clothes at a department store or a factory outlet: You get the same suit in both places, but the factory outlet offers neither assistance nor comfortable surroundings nor free alterations.

Most stockbrokers learn their trade on the job. After they pass a qualifying exam, they receive their broker's license and register with the National Association of Securities Dealers and with the state where they do business.

QUICK TIP: When you interview a broker or money manager, suggests inheritance adviser Michael Alexander of Toronto, ask her to describe the three biggest gains she ever realized and the three biggest losses she ever suffered, and what she learned from these experiences. Ask her for a sample portfolio that displays results over several years (but always bear in mind that past investing success is no guarantee of future success). Ask what her areas of specialization are: If she's the firm's oil and gas specialist, she's likely to encourage you to invest in oil and gas stocks, even if the field is doing poorly. Also, ask whether the firm does its own research or buys it from other sources. If a broker buys information from other firms, she enjoys no particular advantage over the rest of the pack.

FINANCIAL PLANNERS don't invest money for you or recommend specific stocks to buy; they provide more general services, like looking at your whole financial picture, figuring out how best to allocate your assets, advising you about retirement, pension plans, insurance, health care protection, financing college tuitions, etc. If you haven't thought about your financial objectives or goals, a financial planner can help you define them.

Unlike lawyers, accountants, stockbrokers, and money managers, this profession is almost entirely unregulated by any government. But some designations imply a degree of professionalism. **CHARTERED FINANCIAL PLANNER** (CFP) is equivalent to about 18 college semester hours (about one semester) and the passage of a difficult ten-hour exam. **CHARTERED FINANCIAL CONSULTANT** (ChFC) is a lesser designation indicating that the consultant has been trained by the insurance industry. Both of these certificates are relatively easy to obtain and by themselves are not the best measurement of a financial planner's capabilities. Ask financial planners about their educational backgrounds. An undergraduate degree in business is helpful; even better is a master's degree in business administration or in financial planning.

Financial planners work for commissions, fees, or a combination of the two. Most of them are also accountants, stockbrokers, or insurance agents, which means they have a vested interest in pushing some other product or service. Consequently, financial planners have long been regarded as the snake-oil salesmen of the investment advice industry. A notable exception is the "fee-only" financial planner, who collects a flat or hourly fee and has no financial stake in the insurance policies, retirement plans, mutual funds, or other investments she recommends to you. Unfortunately, there are fewer than 1,000 fee-only financial planners in the United States. Look for a member of the National Association of Personal Financial Advisors (NAPFA), whose members are paid a straight fee—no commissions—for their services. NAPFA's toll-free phone line (888-333-6659) or Web site (www.napfa. org) can provide you with a list of its members and a brochure about choosing a financial planner.

DOWNSIDE: The fee-only arrangement provides no performance incentive to the planner; she gets her straight fee whether she serves you well or poorly. Of course, the same is true for most lawyers, accountants and, for that matter, surgeons. What motivates all these professionals is the hope that satisfied customers will provide repeat business in the future.

INSURANCE AGENTS. Your agent should tie all of your insurance together—making sure, for example, that your home owner's policy contains a general liability umbrella clause to protect you in case of lawsuits that arise from accidents on your property.

◆ **Therapists.** Don't laugh. The emotional issues you encounter as an heir will probably far outweigh the financial issues. Unlike wealth you acquire from your business, your labor, or even the lottery, inherited wealth comes to you *only* when someone dies—usually someone to whom you're closely tied. So it's bound to have some emotional impact—and probably a great emotional impact—on you and your relatives, even if you're not consciously aware of it. These emotional issues—especially if you're unaware of them—can undermine the attitudes you need in order to effectively manage your financial responsibilities. Indeed, many of the inheritance issues you believe to be financial will turn out to be emotional when you scratch the surface.

One heiress in the Boston area, for example, was determined to maintain her comfortable lifestyle after her husband's death even though her assets wouldn't have supported her at that level for very long. When her financial planner, Cynthia Coddington, warned her against the dangers of invading her principal, the woman invariably expressed her agreement—but kept on liquidating her capital anyway. Coddington ultimately resigned the client and referred her to a psychologist.

"There was a gap between what she wanted and what she needed, between what she recognized rationally and what drove her emotionally," Coddington explains. "It wasn't so much a matter of managing her finances as managing her expectations. If I can't zero in on someone's insecurities, I don't take the client. I'm a planner, not a psychologist." (In the case of heiress Katherine Gibson, a family therapist helped her sister and parents untangle years of financial noncommunication. See *page 116*.)

A therapist, family counselor, psychologist, or social worker is equipped to help you work out these problems, usually (but not always) for less than you'd pay a lawyer or an accountant. Good therapists, for example, can often heal family rifts in a manner that enables you to avoid lawyers. And sometimes their services are covered by health insurance; check your plan.

Therapists come in all varieties and fee ranges; many specialize in problems of inherited wealth. For references to these, check with some of the inheritors' support groups (see *Resources, page 172*). The most important criterion for choosing a therapist is the sense of rapport you feel with her: If you don't feel comfortable about discussing your innermost feelings, your therapy sessions won't be very helpful.

The best way to find a therapist, suggests family social worker SaraKay Smullens of Philadelphia, is through the recommendation of a friend or relative who has been helped by a therapist in such a way that you can see the positive results for yourself. Your minister or family physician may offer suggestions as well. Or you can seek names of practitioners in your region from one of the following organizations:

National Association of Social Workers, 750 First St. NE, Suite 700, Washington, DC 20002-4241 (202-408-8600). Ask for its register of clinical social workers.

National Council on Family Relations, 3989 Central Ave. NE, Suite 550, Minneapolis, MN 55421 (612-781-9331; also 888-781-9331). Ask for its list of certified family life educators.

American Association for Marriage and Family Therapy, 1133 15th St. NW, Suite 300, Washington, DC 20005-2710 (202-452-0109). This group recommends you look in your local Yellow Pages under "therapists" or "marriage/family/child/individual counselor" and look for names bearing the AAMFT logo.

American Board of Examiners in Clinical Social Work, 21 Merchants Row, Boston, MA 02109 (800-694-5285).

National Registry of Certified Group Psychotherapists, 25 East 21 St., New York, NY 10010 (212-477-1600). (See sidebar, "Financial Solutions Through Family Therapy," on *pages 116–17*.)

TO COMMINGLE ASSETS OR NOT?

Should you combine your inheritance with your other assets? That depends on your situation.

If your marriage is shaky, you might want to keep your inheritance separate from your common household funds or even consider putting it into a trust. That might save you from losing it in a divorce—especially if you live in a "community property" state, where a husband's and wife's holdings are considered "community" (essentially, joint) property unless otherwise specified. In a community property state, it would not be a good idea to commingle the inherited funds with other money unless you specifically wish the inheritance to become community property. The nine community property states are Arizona, California, Idaho, Louisiana, Nevada, New Mexico, Texas, Washington, and Wisconsin.

NOTE: Technically, "community" property and "joint" property aren't the same thing. "Community" means the couple owns all of the household property. "Joint" means each spouse has a half-interest in the household property.

Consult an attorney to see how to keep any money you've inherited separate from your spouse's money or from money that's already commingled.

If you're single, you still might want to keep your inheritance separate from your other funds. For one thing, a sudden dramatic change in your lifestyle might attract fortune-hunters.

Depending on your temperament, you might want to squirrel your inheritance away so it's out of your consciousness. People who live on inherited money often develop a very different sense of money than those who live on earned income. Because they haven't earned the money themselves, they tend to feel less confident about their abilities and less secure about what they'd do if they lost it all. Consequently, they can be more easily swayed by advisers, scrupulous as well as unscrupulous. (After the notorious Wall Street stock manipulator Jay Gould died in 1892, his son George was in turn swindled out of all his millions by rival financiers.)

Some people perform best under pressure. For them, the best answer may be to isolate the inheritance in some manner so as to pretend that it isn't there. Leonard Stern inherited the Hartz Mountain pet foods empire from his father but always behaved as a self-made man: He peddled door-to-door as a boy,

FINANCIAL SOLUTIONS THROUGH FAMILY THERAPY

KATHERINE GIBSON of Blacksburg, Virginia, and her younger sister are fourth-generation heirs to a 19th-century Midwest business fortune, large enough to require a professional family office. When they got together at Easter in 1994, at the ages of 35 and 33, they found themselves discussing their wills. They both realized that whatever they passed on to their children hinged on their parents' estate plans. When they consulted their mother, she readily acknowledged the importance of anticipating her death but avoided discussing specifics. "There was no antagonism, from my mother," Gibson recalls, "just some foot-dragging. All three of us attributed it to inertia in the family office."

What to do? Gibson sought help from Dennis Pearne, an Arlington, Massachusetts, family therapist who specializes in wealth issues. Under his guidance, the sisters, their parents, and their husbands spent a weekend together in a Boston hotel. In the process of airing their feelings, Katherine and her sister discovered that the family office wasn't to blame for the information logjam; instead, their mother still harbored resentments from a long-ago time when her daughters, as six- and eight-year-old girls, had seemed unappreciative about their wealth. The family members also discovered that they felt compelled to run all messages through Katherine's mother instead of talking to each other directly.

"None of us would have identified these things as sources of delay," Katherine Gibson says. "Now our parents were able to hear us express our appreciation to them as adults, not just as the children we were."

From emotional concerns, the discussion moved quickly to financial issues. The daughters discovered that they saw eye-to-eye with their parents on the fundamental issue of trusts. "None of us wanted the children to be controlled from the grave, as we all had been," Gibson says.

As a result of that Boston weekend, their parents subsequently set up a new trust to pay for the education of Katherine's and her sister's children. That's a sound idea because the federal tax code grants an unlimited gift tax exclusion for tuition expenses (although not room and board) paid directly to a school or college. If you figure an average of $10,000 a year tuition for each of the four children, through 16 years of school, that's $640,000 that would otherwise have been subjected to federal gift or inheritance taxes.

Katherine also subsequently set up a trust through which her children will receive a specified dollar amount in three steps, beginning with a small amount at age 18, a larger piece at 25, and the rest at age 40—even though, at that point, Katherine and her husband may still be very much alive. That way, says Gibson, "Our children will have a sense of what's coming to them, but also a sense of limits."

To be sure, Gibson's children may pay a stiff price for their early inheritance. Gibson and her husband are each entitled to give away only $625,000 free of estate or gift taxes (that figure rises to $1 million by the year 2006). They're also each entitled to give each child $10,000 a year—that is, $20,000 per child—tax-free, which the Gibsons have already done for several years. But any amount beyond that will be subject to federal gift tax, which can range from 37 percent to 55 percent. Nevertheless, Gibson says the tax consequences are merely peripheral to her and her husband.

"The estate tax feels to me like a reasonable price to pay for the emotional benefit to our children," she says. And the Gibsons' kids will derive one tax benefit from receiving their inheritance early: The gift tax the children pay upon receiving their payouts will be deducted from their parents' taxable estate when Katherine and her husband die.

earned his bachelor's degree in two and a half years, and picked up his M.B.A. at night while working by day as a $40-a-week clerk in a variety store. Perhaps because of this mindset, Stern subsequently expanded his father's holdings exponentially. Former President George Bush came from a prominent and wealthy Connecticut family, but after college he moved to Texas to break into the wildcat oil business as a beginner in a strange state where he enjoyed no connections.

In effect, Stern and Bush motivated themselves by squirreling away their inheritance and pretending they'd inherited nothing—although, to be sure, in some recess of his mind each man had the luxury of knowing he had an ace in the hole.

REWRITING YOUR OWN WILL

One of the first things your lawyer should do is help you rewrite your own will to take into account the change in assets available, and how you'll ultimately want them distributed. If you've received a large inheritance, that's likely to make your will more complicated than it was previously. Instead of leaving bequests to two children, perhaps you'd now like to leave something to a dozen relatives. If you previously divided your estate among half a dozen favorite charities, perhaps now you want to expand the number to two dozen. If your children are young, perhaps you want to set up a trust for them, at least until they reach adulthood. And if your potential estate exceeds $625,000—the federal estate tax exemption limit (rising to $1 million by 2006)—you'll want to build in protections against estate taxes (see *Part 1, page 33*). (For more on writing a will, see *Part 1, page 43.*)

PART

Handling
NEW WEALTH

F YOU CAME into your inheritance years ago but are still wrestling with inheritance issues, this section is for you.

When Sally Lowell's workaholic husband Ronald suddenly died of a heart attack in 1986, she was 54 and assumed she was a wealthy woman. Ronald had taken over the family company founded by Sally's grandfather—Churchill Linen Service of Brockton, Massachusetts—and built it into one of the Boston region's largest linen suppliers before he retired at age 51 to plunge into various other business enterprises. He created a trust for Sally but never discussed the family's finances with her, and she never asked.

"My parents took care of me, my husband took care of me, and I assumed the bank would take care of me," she says today. "It was my own ignorance."

Actually, Sally's husband had left her about $500,000 in the trust. She also owned a one-third interest—then worth about $300,000—in a land trust she shared equally with her mother and brother. Ronald's businesses also generated a monthly income check for her.

After Ronald died, Sally assuaged her grief by traveling "everywhere," going on cruises and buying what she calls "a fabulous wardrobe." She also paid for her daughter's wedding and finished putting the last of her four children through college. Meanwhile, Ronald's designated trustee— Shawmut Bank—was acquired by Fleet Financial Corp. Between that transition, the complicated nature of Ronald's holdings and Sally's passivity, she became an easy beneficiary for the bank to ignore in the midst of its own transition.

When income checks came to her from Ronald's

businesses, Sally mistakenly forwarded them to the trust officer—one of whom, preoccupied with other, more pressing, concerns, once told her, "I didn't know what to do with it, so I put it in the drawer." After she realized that these checks were hers to spend at her discretion, she tried to invest them on her own, since she didn't trust the bank. "I was buying stocks and managing my own money," she says. "But I really didn't know what I was doing." Sally also suffered tax penalties by dipping into her Individual Retirement Account (IRA) before she reached the age of 59½. "No one told me not to touch it," she says.

Four years after Ronald died, the checks from his businesses stopped; and 10 years after he died, Ronald's estate still hadn't been settled.

Sally eventually got her act together. First she found a lawyer she trusted. He wrapped up the estate and switched her husband's trust from the Fleet Bank to a more responsive trustee at Merrill Lynch, the giant brokerage firm. But by that time—thanks to legal fees (some $78,000) and management fees ($500 a month on the land trust alone), as well as poor investment performance and Sally's profligate spending—the value of her first trust had dwindled to $42,000 and her share of the family land trust was down to $187,000. In 1995, when she was 63, Sally went to work as a bit-part actress in TV commercials and films, including a role as a witch in the 1995 film of *The Crucible.*

"I lived far beyond my means," she says in retrospect. "When your husband dies, so much is going on. I thought I was very wealthy, but I had never dealt with these issues; I only dealt with people in social situations. I'm thrilled that my daughters are working women who know how to deal with institutions. But it's a shame I didn't catch on sooner."

Sally Lowell's case is increasingly rare in an age of working women and easily accessible financial information. But her story demonstrates the critical importance of financial acumen—or, in its absence, the critical importance of good advisers. A sudden financial windfall like an inheritance—especially when it accompanies the emotional blow of the death of a loved one—can be more of a curse than a blessing if you're unprepared for it.

To Barbara Steinmetz, a financial planner in Burlingame, California, Sally Lowell's story suggests several morals:

◆ When it comes to advisers, "You have to kiss a few toads before you meet the handsome prince."

◆ There's no substitute for being on top of your own affairs. You need to watch the people charged with watching your assets.

◆ Even the most ethical advisers, if unchecked, may be tempted to abuse their power.

◆ When it comes to your inheritance, you don't need to know all the answers. But you do need to learn how to ask the right questions. Educating yourself—at least about the vocabulary of finance, so you won't be intimidated the way Sally Lowell was—is crucial.

MANAGING YOUR
DIRECT INHERITANCE

THIS SECTION SEEKS to help you deal with a direct bequest. If all of your inheritance is in a trust, skip this section and proceed to *page 131.*

UTILIZING YOUR PROFESSIONAL ADVISERS

If you lack professional advisers—like a lawyer, accountant, money manager, financial planner, or therapist—see *Part 2, page 102,* for suggestions about how to choose them.

If your advisers are already in place, here are some key points about making the best use of them, mainly provided by lawyers Emily Card and Adam Miller (in their book *Managing Your Inheritance*).

1 Cultivate long-term relationships with advisers you trust. Most professionals will go the extra mile for clients they care about. Conversely, no amount of money can command attention for you if you're perceived as difficult or someone who constantly changes advisers. But recognize that your access to the best advisers depends in part on the size of your assets.

2 Hire and be willing to pay for the services of competent professionals.

3 Delegate authority and don't second-guess. Your advisers will respect you if you keep aware of everything but interfere as little as possible.

4 Allow your advisers to delegate authority.

5 Focus on the big picture rather than details.

6 Be consistent.

7 Don't be a perfectionist.

8 Recognize that complex questions often lack bottom-line answers.

9 Listen to advice and be decisive and timely in your response.

10 Don't push every rule to the limit.

11 Handle as much of the administrative work of running your finances yourself. Save your advisers for the truly complex matters. Remember the old adage: "When you cut your own wood, you warm yourself twice."

12 Recognize that life involves trade-offs, and take responsibility for your choices.

13 Use advisers as gatekeepers to those seeking investments and contributions from you.

14 Plan and work in weeks, months, and years rather than in minutes, hours, and days.

15 Follow through in a timely fashion.

16 If you'll be on vacation or hard to locate, give a limited power of attorney for the time you'll be away. This can allow your adviser to move ahead on deadlines within the parameters you have established. (Don't give a general power of attorney, which gives your

adviser the right to act as your proxy on all matters at all times.)

17 Be aware of a professional's time constraints and plan ahead.

18 Only use demanding deadlines when it's necessary.

19 Keep good professionals.

20 Encourage open and informal communication with your advisers.

21 Courtesy and tact are free; use them even when you're footing the bill.

22 Hold regular planning meetings with your professional team, even if only once every two or three years. These meetings develop your relationship, allow open communication, and enable brainstorming. Come prepared. Read all the materials your advisers have prepared for you in advance. Write down specific questions. That way you don't waste their time—and your money.

INVESTING

Before you think about investing, make sure your bases are covered. Ask yourself these basic questions:

Does your income exceed your expenses?

Are you saving at least 10 percent of your take-home pay? That's what you'll need for your retirement if you start saving from ground zero in your 30s. You'll need more if you start later.

Do you have an emergency fund to cover unexpected expenses like a sudden illness or major repairs to your house or car? Such a fund should contain two to six months' living expenses and be kept in a readily available place, like a bank savings account or a money market fund with check-writing privileges. That way, when an emergency arises you can gain access to the money without touching retirement funds or other investments.

Do you have adequate insurance to protect you and your dependents from major financial losses such as death, disability, medical catastrophes, theft, or the destruction of your property?

If these bases are covered, then you're ready to think about investing whatever excess funds you have. The more solid your foundation—assets like your house, life insurance, bank accounts, money market funds—the more discretion you have to make riskier investments in stocks and bonds.

Investing basically involves three strategies, none of which is mutually exclusive of the others:

1 Compounding. The simplest way to make assets grow is by reinvesting the dividends and interest. Financial columnist Jane Bryant Quinn notes that if you invested $100 in a typical stock at the end of 1926 and reinvested all the dividends, by the end of 1990 the investment would be worth $55,000. By contrast, if you spent all the dividend payments over that period, in 1990 your investment would be worth only $3,000. Of course, this strategy requires patience and sacrifice—two human characteristics in extremely short supply.

2 Asset allocation. This is simply a term for the way you divide your investments among the three major categories: stocks, bonds, and cash or cash equivalents (checking accounts and money market funds). How you allocate your assets depends largely on your age. Younger investors tend to invest more in aggressive (albeit risky) stocks with strong growth potential. Older investors, hoping to generate steady income and preserve their capital for their retirement, tend to put more money in less risky (but also less rewarding) cash and bonds.

3 Diversification. Where will your money make the most money? To the 19th-century steel magnate Andrew Carnegie, the answer was simple: "Put all your eggs in one basket—and watch that basket." Yet a century later, the 1981 Nobel prize laureate economist James Tobin provided an equally simple—and entirely opposite—answer: "Don't put all your eggs in one basket." Nineteenth-century investors assumed that if every asset within an investment portfolio was suitable, the overall portfolio would be suitable, too. But from the 1950s onward, economists discovered that you could construct an even more suitable portfolio by putting together individual assets that, taken alone, might be quite unsuitable.

For example: An unexpected increase in the price of oil will cause most oil stocks to rise and most airline stocks to decline because airlines depend heavily on oil. Thus oil stocks and airline stocks taken individually may be risky investments. But if you balance them together in a single portfolio, oil and airline stocks may provide a relatively attractive return with only moderate risk.

This theory of diversification holds that you are best off spreading your risks across a variety of stocks, bonds, and cash, across a variety of types of stocks, and even a variety of countries. In effect, you increase your opportunities for profit while decreasing your exposure to risk. Mutual funds—which pool the investments of thousands of investors—offer the best vehicle for diversification. But it's a good idea to diversify your mutual fund investments, too.

If you're new to investing, you probably need professional help or at least a good basic manual. (For more on choosing investment advisers, money managers, stockbrokers, etc., see *Part 2, pages 109–12.* For some suggested reading, see *Resources, pages 184–85.*)

IF YOU'RE A SURVIVING SPOUSE

If you're a surviving spouse, you may find yourself in conflict with middle-aged children or stepchildren whose expectations don't match their earning power. You may feel guilty about receiving a large lump sum from your late spouse while your own children or stepchildren are struggling financially. In such a situation, you may be tempted to help your children buy a house or pay for private school tuitions. But this is a risky strategy unless you're self-sufficient and enjoy good earning power of your own. For your children's sake as well as your own, your first priority must be to protect yourself and preserve your inheritance. Remember: Americans nowadays increasingly outlive their incomes. You need to conserve your funds so you won't run short if you should need a life-care facility. Otherwise, the burden of caring for you in your old age may very well fall on your children.

But you ask: What are parents and children for, if not to care for each other in time of need? How can you protect yourself against your future nursing home expenses or catastrophic illness and still help out your children? One answer is to create an irrevocable trust or a gift-giving program. Such a trust could provide for distribution of some of the trust's income as gifts to your children, with the principal to be used for your medical or nursing home expenses. Anything left over in the trust after you die could be passed on to your children.

Another suggestion, from financial planner Tom Batterman of Wausau, Wisconsin: Specify, either in your will or in a trust document, that a specific fraction of your estate will go to your stepchildren and the rest to your own biological children. Advise your children and stepchildren that you've taken this step. This makes it clear to them that you've provided for them; it also gives them a common interest in the health of your estate.

These are merely two possibilities. Whether such tactics will work in your particular case remains to be seen. Batterman himself says that in cases of remarriages, there's no such thing as an ideal solution. "Not a lot can keep stepchildren and stepparents on good terms," he says. "I can't think of one case where the relationships didn't blow apart later in life."

To tailor a program to your individual situation,

consult a lawyer or financial planner. (For more on irrevocable trusts, see *Part 1, page 50.*)

PLANNING YOUR OWN ESTATE

If you don't have a will, or your will hasn't been updated for many years, see your lawyer or financial planner and have this taken care of immediately. If you fail to plan your estate or leave a will, the court will do the job for you—distributing your property according to a formula specified by state law, choosing a guardian for your children, and selecting an administrator. Each state's intestacy laws determine who'll receive what portion of your estate. Generally, spouses receive one-third to one-half of the estate, and children divide the rest. If you have no spouse or children, all your assets could wind up in the state treasury.

If you're ready to proceed with a will or an estate plan, see *Part 1*. The advice about helping your parents plan their estates applies to you as well. Also see *Part 2, page 118.*

LIVING WITH AN
IRREVOCABLE TRUST

YEARS AGO YOUR PARENTS or your spouse created a trust for your benefit. (For the mechanics of setting up a trust, see *Part 1, pages 50–82.*) The trust creator has been dead for years, and you may be getting on in years yourself. But the trust persists, making no allowance for the fact that you're no longer a child. This section offers advice on coping with this often frustrating situation.

YOUR GOALS AS A TRUST BENEFICIARY

A trust is administered by a trustee for your benefit, but you're not his sole concern. He must also answer to the needs of other beneficiaries and (if he works for a bank or corporate trust company) the needs of his employer's bottom line—goals that may conflict with yours. Your first order of business is to understand precisely what goals you want the trust to deliver for you:

1 Maximum return and/or growth on the assets in the trust.

2 Fair but not excessive management fees for the trustee.

3 You should receive the full income amount due you each year.

4 All the beneficiaries should be treated equitably.

5 The trustee must operate honestly.

Achieving these goals requires three basic commodities: information, brains, and advice.

YOUR RIGHTS TO INFORMATION ABOUT THE MANAGEMENT OF YOUR TRUST

If you're a beneficiary of a trust, in most cases you have a right to know what the trust is doing with your assets, even if you have only a minor interest. Here are the key documents you should ask to see:

The **TRUST DOCUMENT**. Pay close attention to the trust's discretionary language. For example, a trust document may instruct the trustee to provide you with sufficient funds to live in your "customary lifestyle." But the trustee may not understand what this means— in which case you may need to enlighten him.

The **QUARTERLY** or **MONTHLY TRUST REPORT**. In particular, keep yourself informed about distributable net income. Be sure that the income due you is disbursed each year in full. If it's left in the trust to accumulate, that undistributed income will typically be taxed as income to the trust and then added to the trust's principal. That means it won't be available for your use unless the trust document specifically allows for its distribution.

DEALING WITH TRUSTEES

The trustee's function is to administer a trust for the benefit of all the beneficiaries—the income beneficiaries as well as the remainder interests. In practice, beneficiaries usually have no legal say in how a trust is managed. When a bank trustee mismanages an account, raises fees arbitrarily, or sweeps assets into the bank's own proprietary mutual funds, beneficiaries often find themselves powerless to resist, short of going to court—because the trust creator is dead and the document he left behind is irrevocable. Nor is going to court a viable option, because most trust agreements say the trustee can dip into the trust's assets to pay for his legal defense. (See the case of John Upp in *Part 1, page 76.*)

"Banks technically make money from loans," says Philadelphia plaintiff's lawyer Richard Greenfield, "but in the last 10 to 15 years, they're under pressure to make money from fee income. Those banks with trust powers have this piggy bank to reach into." Although most banks charge a percent of principal (usually 1.5 percent to 2.5 percent, and less on very large accounts) as a basic annual management fee, many trust agreements contain a provision allowing the trustee to adjust its management fees "as the need may arise from time to time." That, Greenfield contends, is "a license to steal."

In one egregious case, in 1992 Philadelphia-based CoreStates Bank imposed an extra annual $600 fee on all trusts in excess of $50,000 for what it called "regulatory compliance compensation," even though the cost of complying with government regulations was already part of the bank's general overhead. Only after angry beneficiaries filed a class-action suit did CoreStates discontinue the charge and refund the fees collected.

In the past, such grievances concerned only the rich and consequently attracted little public attention. But trusts have now become a middle-class financial instrument as well. Some trusts are as small as $10,000, and the median value of the 950,000 personal trusts administered by financial institutions reporting to fed-

CASE HISTORIES: "PRISONERS" OF TRUSTS

TO MOST RESIDENTS of Charlotte, North Carolina, in 1995, Herman Moore Jr. was a member of the local establishment: At 65 he was, among other things, a former president pro tem of the North Carolina Senate and an old friend of NationsBank chief executive Hugh McCall. But to his trustee at NationsBank, Moore was merely one of several beneficiaries of a 49-year-old trust that wouldn't expire until the death of Moore's mother, then 89 (and still living at this writing). That year, after going through five trust officers in eight years, Moore and his relatives sued NationsBank for mismanagement and fraud. Among other things, they alleged that back in the high-interest-rate days of late 1970s, when money market funds were yielding 20 percent returns, the bank blew an opportunity to borrow against the trust's life insurance policies at 5 percent, thereby costing the trust hundreds of thousands of dollars in interest income. The bank has offered to settle for "more than we'd probably win," Moore has said, but Moore insists the money is beside the point. "I want an admission of guilt," he says. "Or I want to see them convicted."

Or consider the quandary of Gary Marbut of Missoula, Montana, a law school graduate and investor who has himself served as trustee of several estates. Since 1956 Marbut's wife—the granddaughter of Frank Mitchell Eaton, cofounder of the Eaton Corp.—has been a beneficiary of family trusts worth about $5 million and administered by the Colorado National Bank. In 1985, the family became concerned that the

eral regulators is only about $450,000, according to one estimate.

Internal Revenue Service data suggest that about 2.8 million Americans are designated income beneficiaries of personal trusts, and perhaps three times that number are "remainders"—the children or grandchildren who will receive the trust assets after the trust terminates. And that means that on any given day some 11

bank was making bad investments, paying unnecessary taxes, and charging excessive fees. The relatives elected Marbut to approach the bank, and he persuaded the bank to let him act as the trust's *de facto* portfolio manager. The bank, he reports, was so pleased with his investment performance that it applied his ideas to other accounts.

But then Colorado National was merged into First Bank Systems of Minneapolis, which refused to let Marbut pick stocks except from the inventory of the bank's own mutual funds. First Bank Systems also refused to provide data on its long-term investment performance. At the same time, Marbut says he found that the bank's fees had risen to a point where they approached 30 percent of the trust's income.

In a series of meetings and letters, the bank refused to alter its policy, adjust its fees, or resign as trustee. In one letter to Marbut in 1996, a bank senior vice-president cavalierly explained that, among other reasons, the bank could not resign as trustee because of "the long and satisfactory relationship the bank has had with your family. . . . To terminate this relationship would be as difficult for us as it would for your family."

"They're looking through the telescope from the wrong end," says Marbut . "Our relationship has not been satisfactory, but that doesn't seem to concern them." When Marbut filed suit in December 1997, the bank had been merged and renamed once again: Now the defendant called itself U.S. Bank, formerly of Portland, Oregon.

million Americans are affected by irrevocable trusts.

It also means that many trust beneficiaries are not idle dandies clipping coupons in the Bahamas, but accomplished and mature adults—perhaps like you—who chafe at an arrangement that treats them like perpetual children (see the sidebar, *above*).

Bankers claim that it's the beneficiaries who have things backwards. To bankers, a trustee performs a thankless job that involves fulfilling the wishes of the deceased person who created the trust (called the grantor or settlor) while reconciling the fractious interests of living beneficiaries, not to mention some remainders who may not even have been born yet. The purpose of a trust, argues Dan Reisteter, director of government relations for the Pennsylvania Bankers Association, "is to carry out the wishes of the settlor, not the beneficiary."

"The real issue," says David Officer, executive vice-president of Pittsburgh-based Mellon Bank, one of the nation's largest trust operations, "is between income beneficiaries who want more money now and remaindermen who'll get the money in the future." The trustee, he suggests, often becomes a scapegoat for beneficiaries' anger toward their dead parents. "Who decided to treat them like children?" Officer asks rhetorically. "It was the grantor. The beneficiaries are really irritated that they have to go hat in hand to someone else—but that's not our fault."

If beneficiaries could change a trustee at will, Reisteter adds, then the settlor would have no assurance that her wishes will be carried out after her death. But the trouble with that logic, reformers argue, is that most settlors don't really know what they want in the first place.

"Lawyers presume the settlor understood what he signed," says law professor Robert Whitman of the University of Connecticut. "But tax-driven documents cannot be understood by ordinary people, or even by 80 percent of the bar."

Beneficiaries began fighting back in 1991 when 15 unhappy heirs gathered on Philadelphia's Main Line to swap horror stories. A *Philadelphia Inquirer* report of that meeting generated 160 inquiries, and from that nucleus the support group known as Heirs Inc. was born. Today the group provides its 2,000-person mailing list with moral support and advice, publishes a newsletter and personal trust handbook, lobbies for legislation on behalf of beneficiaries, sponsors an annual conference in Palm Beach, and tries to wield its bargaining power to promote user-friendly trust arrangements. Heirs Inc. members dressed in Santa Claus suits even picketed the offices of Bankers Trust Company in New York City in December 1996 to publicize a member's complaints.

Its media coverage notwithstanding, Heirs Inc. is largely a one-man band that operates out of the Villanova, Pennsylvania, basement of Standish H. Smith, its ebullient and energetic leader. Like many another unhappy beneficiary, Smith readily acknowledges that his grievances are both financial and psychological. After his mother-in-law died in 1976, Smith, then 44, gave up his careers as a systems analyst and a restorer of classic cars to focus on his wife's trust. He naively assumed that the trustee, Girard Bank (now Mellon Bank), would treat him as a customer, much the way a brokerage treats a client.

"I thought, 'I'm the head of this family; I should be part of the financial equation,'" he recalls. "But Girard laughed at me. They said, 'We have title to this account—you're out of the loop.' That's what annoyed me." In addition to his time, Smith now contributes some $15,000 to Heirs Inc.'s annual $35,000 budget; what he gets in exchange is a power trip. "It's fun," he says. "We have to continue to sue the pants off these guys. They'll never come to the table in a reasonable manner."

The beneficiaries' newfound militance is behind some recent reforms in state laws, where virtually all trust activity is regulated. California, for example, has added several new grounds for removing a trustee, including excessive fees—although the burden of proof is still on the petitioner. Under a bill currently pending in the Pennsylvania legislature, beneficiaries of a trust could switch trustees without cause just by voting among themselves to do so. In Florida, a trustee now has the burden of proving the reasonableness of his fees, and beneficiaries can inspect records and require periodic accountings.

The national Uniform Trust Act, which provides a model for state trust codes, recently added language stating that "Trusts are created primarily to benefit beneficiaries." Reform efforts are also under way in Indiana, Oklahoma, and New Hampshire. And since 1995 the Internal Revenue Service has permitted the creator of a trust to include a clause allowing beneficiaries to remove a problem trustee. (Previously the IRS maintained that a beneficiary who possessed the power to change a trustee effectively controlled the trust assets, in which case the assets should be included in his taxable estate.)

Whether these developments represent progress is another question. Once income beneficiaries enjoy the power to remove a trustee, for example, in effect they gain leverage over the remaindermen—some possibly unborn—who will ultimately inherit the trust's assets. "A beneficiary could say to the trustee, 'If you don't give me more money, I'm moving the account,'" says David Officer of Mellon Bank. "I have a real problem with that." Even Professor Whitman of the University of Connecticut, a champion of beneficiaries who has been circulating a proposed "Beneficiaries' Bill of Rights" among trust companies without much success, sees legislation and lawsuits as ineffective ways to advance beneficiaries' interests. "This thing will be solved when reasonable people sit down and come up with reasonable solutions," he says.

Actually, the tensions between beneficiaries and banks are already resolving themselves through the competitive pressures of a radically changing marketplace. New players, like investment houses, brokerage houses, and independent (non-bank) trust companies are increasingly challenging banks' traditional domination of personal trust business. Bank of Bermuda (N.Y.) Ltd., for example, offers a proposed trust agreement that provides for its own removal as trustee by action of the beneficiaries. Bank mergers may have wiped out countless small and friendly banks, but they've also wiped out the cozy relationships between banks and lawyers that produced many onerous trust documents in the past.

"Our competition today is much more from Merrill Lynches and Fidelity Trusts—not from other banks," says Officer of Mellon Bank. "And clients are more sophisticated now than they were 10 years ago. New clients won't come in unless you perform." And changes in tax laws now limit the benefits available from generation-skipping trusts (see *Part 1, page 63*), with the result that most trusts created today are much shorter in duration. Nevertheless, a typical trust is still designed to provide income to the surviving spouse and the residual estate to the couple's children after the spouse's death.

But these developments are cold comfort if you're an unhappy beneficiary who is held hostage to a trust set up a generation ago or longer. In that case, the challenge before you is difficult, but not always impossible.

IMPROVING YOUR TRUSTEE'S PERFORMANCE
A trustee basically fulfills two functions: administration and money management. (Sometimes he delegates the money management to another party, or just invests all the assets in an index mutual fund.) As the beneficiary of an irrevocable trust, your interests are best served if you get the best possible performance in both these functions. But your challenge is to get along, possibly for years, with a trustee whose ideas and objectives may be diametrically opposed to your own. A bank trustee is legally required as a fiduciary to balance demands for *present income* for the benefit of the income beneficiaries against the need to encourage

future asset growth for the benefit of the remainders'
interests. He also needs, of course, to operate your
trust in a manner that makes a profit for the bank. So
if you have complaints about your trustee, they're most
likely to fall into one of these categories:

◆ The trust assets and your income from the trust
aren't keeping pace with inflation or growing as fast as
you think they should.

◆ The trustee's management fees and expenses are
rising or seem unjustified.

◆ The trustee refuses to touch the principal in order
to give you money you need in an emergency, even
though the trust document allows distributions for
medical or educational purposes or even for your general living expenses.

◆ The trustee has touched the principal to give emergency money to another beneficiary, thereby diluting
your share.

◆ The trustee is self-dealing—for example, commin-
gling trust assets with the trustee's assets, selling trust
assets to his friends or relatives for less than their market value, or voting a block of the trust's stock in a
company in which the trustee owns a controlling
interest.

◆ The trustee doesn't provide you with reassuring
answers to your questions.

All of these are valid concerns on your part. But in
most of them you have no legal recourse. Poor investment performance or snooty behavior, for example,
doesn't constitute sufficient legal grounds to have a
trustee removed unless the trust document
specifically says so.

So in most cases, coexistence—not confrontation—
is your best bet, because without a trustee removal
clause, technically you are powerless to influence the
trust's distributions, investments, or fees—or to
remove the trustee. But trustees are human—yes, even

those who work for bank trust departments. They'd rather have you happy than angry, and they'd rather have you recommending their bank to your friends instead of denouncing it. And they'd rather deal with someone who's informed than someone who's ignorant. If you know what you're talking about and stick up for yourself, they're likely to respond. If you act helpless, they're more likely to treat you that way.

"When the inevitable questions are raised regarding the trustee's performance, as beneficiaries are apt to do, it is essential that they know what constitutes good trust management and have sufficient leverage to insure that decisions are made solely with their interests in mind," says Standish Smith, president of Heirs Inc., the beneficiaries' support group.

"When you go after a trustee for bad management," says beneficiary Rick Adams of New York, himself a former senior vice president at Merrill Lynch, "you win if you get rid of him, and you win if you keep him—because you whipped him into shape." Adams succeeded in getting his Philadelphia-based trust moved from Girard Bank (now Mellon Bank) to Glenmede Trust Company, a more beneficiary-friendly trustee.

To whip your trustee into shape, try some of the following tactics:

OBTAIN AND KEEP COPIES OF IMPORTANT PAPERS: operative trust instruments, accounting statements, correspondence with trustees, and fiduciary tax returns.

READ AND UNDERSTAND YOUR TRUST DOCUMENTS AND PERIODIC ACCOUNT STATEMENTS. If you can't understand them, find a professional adviser (see *Part 2, page 102*), or turn to a beneficiaries' support group (see *Resources, page 172*). The best way to monitor a trustee's performance and fees is to dissect the trust statements. Unsatisfactory performance or incomplete information should be brought to the trustee's attention. But bear in mind that the trustee may be hamstrung by your parents' requirements.

DEVELOP A GOOD RELATIONSHIP WITH YOUR TRUST OFFICER. Your physical presence helps remind him whose money it is: yours. Remember: Legally, the assets are held by the trustee in trust for the beneficiaries. Communicate regularly with your trust officer; meet with him if necessary, and memorialize important matters in follow-up letters, retaining copies for yourself.

MAKE A LIST OF YOUR COMPLAINTS. Analyze and prioritize them. Ask yourself which ones are really important to you. Remember the story of the boy who cried wolf: If you pick up the phone and call your trustee for every slight complaint, you'll undermine your credibility when a truly serious problem comes along.

DOCUMENT EVERYTHING. After you talk to the trustee, send him a letter confirming the conversation. One woman used her notes as leverage to get her trustee replaced. Another wrote so many letters to her trustee that the trustee asked her to find another trustee—which was just what she'd hoped he would do. Use certified mail, return receipt requested, if you need to create a paper trail.

RETAIN A GOOD ATTORNEY AND ACCOUNTANT to review matters, advise you, and to press your case with the trustee from time to time. (For how to choose an attorney, see *Part 2, page 107*.) Trustees who resist change might be swayed by an outsider. You might use an investment adviser also. (See *Part 2, page 109*, for how to choose one.) But note: Standard investment advice often doesn't apply in a trust situation, because of the need to satisfy both current and future beneficiaries.

IF YOU THINK YOU'VE BEEN SHORT-CHANGED, or if you need money for an emergency or a special purpose (say, to finance a business or a house), contact your trustee. If you don't get satisfaction, a lawyer can review your trust document to see if there is any flexibility in managing and distributing the assets. (See sidebar, right.)

A CASE HISTORY: HELP FROM A PRO

WHEN JOHN BREWER died in 1983, he left $250,000 in a trust set up for his wife, Elizabeth. His local suburban Philadelphia bank was designated as trustee. As time passed, Elizabeth grew frustrated with the bank's high fees and inflexibility. When she wanted to buy a new home, for example, the bank refused to let her pledge the assets in the trust as collateral for a loan.

The trust document prohibited her from switching trustees, but in the early 1990s she hired a lawyer who studied the document for other options. He discovered that, in addition to her annual income from the trust, she was entitled to take out a small portion of the principal periodically, thanks to a so-called "five-and-five" provision allowing removal of $5,000 or 5 percent of the principal, whichever is greater. So in 1992 she began removing $5,000 annually from the trust—the maximum permitted—and placing it in mutual funds of her own choosing. "I was determined to regain some control," she said—and she has.

WHEN YOU HAVE A COMPLAINT, TELL YOUR TRUSTEE. If you don't complain, the trustee is more likely to conclude that she can get away with almost anything.

WHEN YOU VOICE COMPLAINTS, DON'T GET HYSTERICAL. Approach your trustee as if you're a consumer with a legitimate concern. Work from a non-confrontational stance, using facts and logic rather than emotion to make your points. Treat your trustee with respect; try to see his point of view. Your real quarrel may lie not with him but with your parents, who created the trust document that your trustee is bound to follow.

DON'T BE SHY ABOUT NEGOTIATING TRUSTEE FEES. Research the typical trustee rates at your local banks, brokerage houses, and independent corporate trustees (such as private trust companies). If they're lower than what your trust pays, mention it to your trustee and demand an explanation. Sometimes the power of embarrassment works wonders. The larger the trust, the more room for negotiation.

BE PERSISTENT. If you reach a stalemate with your trustee, return again at a future date.

STAY IN TOUCH WITH OTHER BENEFICIARIES and share information with them.

SAVE ALL OF YOUR TRUSTEE'S COMMUNICATIONS. If you ever need to take him to court, these papers could show premeditated pattern of misbehavior on the trustee's part.

JOIN A SUPPORT GROUP like Heirs Inc. (Box 292, Villanova, PA 19085; 610-525-4442) or Resourceful Women (1016 Thoreau Center, Second floor, P.O. Box 29423, San Francisco, CA 94129-0423; 415-561-6520) or The Impact Project (21 Linwood St., Arlington, MA 02174; 781-648-0776). Sometimes these organizations can negotiate with a trust institution as a group, which can give you more leverage.

SUBSCRIBE TO A NEWSLETTER like *Family Money* (1515 Fourth St., Suite B, Napa, CA 94559; Judy G. Barber, publisher; 707-255-6254) or *Fiduciary Fun*, published by Heirs Inc.

◆ **Checking investment performance.** The mere fact that your trust assets and income increase each year isn't cause for rejoicing. In an inflationary economy, positive results alone aren't sufficient; the growth must exceed the inflation rate. If you depend on the income from your trust to meet much of your living expenses, each year your trust must produce more income just to maintain the same purchasing power that you enjoyed the previous year. If your assets and income increased by 3 percent last year but inflation jumped by 5 percent, you actually suffered a 2 percent loss for the year.

Checking your trust's portfolio performance is a relatively easy matter. Simply compare the percentage change in the Consumer Price Index (CPI) with the percentage change in the value of your trust's overall securities. The CPI is available on a monthly basis from the U.S. Commerce Department or any public library. There's a national as well as a regional CPI, but the percentage change in both is usually similar.

If your trust portfolio's percentage change is substantially greater than the change in the CPI and the trust hasn't added significant new principal to its assets, then the trust portfolio is at least keeping pace with inflation, which means you'll be able to maintain your present lifestyle. But if your trust portfolio's percentage change is the same or less than the percentage change in the CPI—and if the trustee hasn't made substantial subtractions from the assets—query your trustee for an explanation. If the trust's investment performance doesn't improve, you may be forced to tighten your belt. Do-it-yourself charts for making such comparisons are available from Heirs Inc.

NOTE: Remember, if you've been taking significant amounts out of your trust principal—say, to buy a house or a car—the percentage growth of your trust will be reduced and it will *appear* to have performed worse than it actually did. In cases where the trust principal has been added to or subtracted from, use this exercise for a clearer picture: From the trust statements, estimate the total of all payments over the years from the trust *principal,* and deduct from that any additions to principal (in cash or securities, but not real estate). This will give you a clearer (although not perfect) estimate of what the value of your trust would have been as of last December 31st if you'd never touched the principal. This result, compared against the CPI increase for that year, will enable you to see whether your trust is staying ahead of inflation.

Here are general investment guidelines for trustees:

The trustee's investments must follow the requirements of the trust document, assuming those requirements are legal.

A corporate fiduciary is held to a higher standard than an individual trustee.

Investment standards vary from state to state. Nineteen states require a fiduciary to behave as a "prudent man" would—that is, striving above all to preserve the capital value of each investment and avoid risk. This rule dates back to 1830, but since the 1950s it has been amply demonstrated that such a strategy is actually imprudent in a surging economy. (An investment in the Standard & Poor's 500 Stock Index over five or 10 years will almost certainly outperform the return from U.S. Treasury notes—even though, since the stock market rises and falls, on any given day the T-bills may perform better than stocks.) Consequently, today 31 states plus the District of Columbia follow the more flexible "prudent investor" rule, which focuses on the health of the entire portfolio over the long run.

Poor or even failed investments by a trustee aren't grounds for removal or legal action unless malfeasance is involved.

◆ **Challenging management fees.** Most older trust documents set no limits on management fees; instead they simply authorize the trust (if it's a bank) to charge according to its standard fee schedule. As plaintiffs' lawyers have pointed out, this amounts to a license to steal for the banks. On the other hand, the federal courts have established the principle that the trustee's first obligation is to the interests of the beneficiaries. The fees charged by a bank or other trustee can directly affect the beneficiaries' welfare—for example, if management fees are eating up most of the trust's income, so that the trustee earns more from the trust than the beneficiaries do. Thus you have a legal as well as a moral basis to demand that a trustee's fees be reasonable in terms of the services provided, and even in terms of the trust's investment performance or the cost of administration. If this issue comes to court, the burden of proof is on the bank to justify its charges—

and this mere knowledge offers leverage you can apply without going to court.

Since fees vary from bank to bank and even from trust to trust within a bank (generally, the larger the trust, the lower the percentage administrative fee), you may be able to exercise some moral leverage.

◆ **Is your trustee ripping you off?** Look for the tell-tale signs: If your trustee says, "I don't want to bother you with details; it will only confuse you," that's a signal that there may be some impropriety. Or it may mean there's something that another beneficiary doesn't want the trustee to tell you—a sign that the trustee is favoring one beneficiary over you.

If the trustee ignores a question or fails to answer responsively, you may have hit a sensitive area. Repeat the question in further letters, and save copies of each letter. If you continue to receive no reply, you have grounds for concern. You also have documentation in your letters file that the trustee failed to provide the information you requested.

Check your statements and your IRS 1041 fiduciary return for unusual or unexplained expenses.

SETTLING DISPUTES: CONFRONTATIONAL TACTICS

◆ **Going semi-public.** If you've exhausted all efforts at accommodation with your trustee, confrontational tactics may be necessary. But even in such a case, litigation is messy, expensive, emotionally taxing, and should be pursued only as an absolute last resort. (The 1993 check suit by the Roadway Services heirs Tom and George Roush against their bank trustee generated more than 300,000 documents, consuming 120 feet of shelf space, in its first year alone; see *Part 1, page 78*). One possible alternative: Consider contacting other beneficiaries whose trusts are managed by the same trustee. Hold a conference at which all of you can share your experiences about the trustee—and make sure the trustee knows about the conference. The bank's mere knowledge that these people are talking to each other may elicit some action from the bank.

Another alternative: Contact a beneficiaries' support group like Heirs Inc. or Resourceful Women (see addresses on *page 172*). Sometimes there's strength (and ingenuity) in numbers. Resourceful Women, for example, publishes a directory of approved banks and trust companies. When it receives complaints, it confronts the trust officers and removes them from the directory if the complaints continue. That tactic can provide leverage for addressing your complaint. Resourceful Women's plans for the future include an on-line dialogue among trust professionals, lawyers, and beneficiaries, which would make such a complaint process even faster and more effective.

◆ **Going public.** Since banks abhor bad publicity, sometimes the threat of going public with your complaint can rectify the problem, especially if illegal behavior is involved. It might even cause the trustee to step down, especially if your trust is unprofitable to the bank. Fighting requires time and money, and no trust officer wants the world to hear that his investments were up only 4 percent while the market was up 14 percent. Banks are well aware that the mass media hunger constantly for good stories—especially for dramatic tales of conflict between large institutions (like a bank trustee) and helpless individuals (presumably like you). In a criminal case, media exposure can prod a prosecutor to take action.

Concert pianist Suzanne McCormick of Dobbs Ferry, New York, claiming that a trust created for her benefit by her late husband had been mismanaged by Bankers Trust Company, induced several relatives and fellow heirs to picket Bankers Trust's New York City office with her during the 1996 Christmas season, dressed in Santa Claus suits and carrying signs proclaiming, "Don't trust Bankers Trust." The stunt gained her publicity in several newspapers and may have been a factor in the bank's subsequent offer of a multimillion-dollar settlement.

But be wary: To attract the attention of a newspaper columnist or TV reporter, you must have a simple and dramatic horror story that can apply to others besides you.

Ideal sample story: For years the trustee, a major local bank, has been systematically embezzling hundreds of thousands of dollars from your trust to buy a villa in Spain, as a result of which you and your family lost your beloved family mansion—and under the terms of the trust there's nothing you can do about it.

Bad sample story: Your trustee accidentally disbursed a $500 income check to your brother that should have gone to you.

The first example contains drama, greed, malice, villains, victims, and outrage on a huge scale—ideal ingredients for a newspaper column. The second example is merely a minor accident that concerns nobody but your immediate family.

WARNING: Blackmail—which is essentially what the threat of media exposure is—works only if you keep the closet closed. Once you take your story to the local newspaper, the trustee has every incentive to fight back vigorously.

◆ **Going to the government.** Banks are regulated by three federal agencies, and banks may bend over backwards to avoid complaints filed with these agencies. Your letter to one of these agencies—or even the mere suggestion to your bank trust officer that you're thinking of contacting a federal agency—may cause your trust officer to take the path of least resistance and do things your way. Be sure to give your bank the chance to discuss your problem before you fire off a letter to Washington. But if events have left you no alternative but to contact the feds, here are the appropriate contacts.

For nationally chartered banks:
Office of the Controller of the Currency
250 E St. NW
Mail Stop 7-9
Washington, DC 20219
(202-874-4852)

For state-chartered banks that are insured by the Federal Deposit Insurance Corporation (FDIC) and belong to the Federal Reserve System:
Trust & Electronic Data Processing
20th and C Sts. NW
Mail Stop 205
Washington, DC 20551
(202-452-2717)

For state-chartered banks that don't belong to the Federal Reserve System:
FDIC Trust Examiner
Room F-612
550 17th St. NW
Washington, DC 20429
(202-898-6762)

◆ **Suing a trustee.** When a beneficiary sues a trustee, it's usually for one of three reasons:
1 To collect damages for a perceived wrong, especially an act of self-dealing;
2 To challenge the trustee's fees and force a readjustment;
3 To replace the trustee.

Before you take the extreme step of hiring a lawyer and filing a lawsuit, make sure you understand your objective—and also make sure you've weighed the value of the objective against the financial and emotional costs of going to court.

Some beneficiaries believe they can achieve their objectives by threatening to sue without actually filing suit. But such a threat is worthless unless the other side believes you'll follow through. To wage a successful lawsuit—or to achieve your goals without filing suit— you need leverage and credibility. You must assemble as much information as you can to convince the bank's trust officers that they'll lose a suit; that they'll suffer public embarrassment in the process; and that they won't be able to recoup their legal fees from your trust, which they can do if they win.

When you threaten to sue, the bank sizes you up as a potential legal adversary: Are you prepared to litigate? Are you prepared for publicity exposing you to the world as an heir? They know you're probably afraid to have your situation publicized, so they know you won't sue.

Before you sue, ask yourself: "Is it worth the time, the money, and the emotional cost? Is the trustee really the cause of my unhappiness, or am I fighting demons of the past—like my parents, who created this trust because they didn't trust me?" In short, do you have a valid legal case, or are you just looking for emotional satisfaction?

"If you think you'll achieve happiness by hiring a lawyer to beat up on someone, hire a mugger," suggests San Francisco lawyer Dominic Campisi, an authority on trust litigation. "It's much cheaper."

How do you get the other side to believe you'll follow through? Hiring a trust litigator—as opposed to a lawyer who simply drafts trusts and wills—enhances your credibility. A plaintiffs' lawyer takes cases on a contingency basis, which indicates that she's confident of victory. A lawyer who charges an hourly fee is less credible: The bank knows you don't want to spend a lot on legal fees.

◆ **Removing your trustee.** Until recently it was all but impossible to remove a trustee. Even today, in most cases, unless all heirs—including remainders, who inherit money only after the primary beneficiaries die—are in complete agreement, beneficiaries of a trust must go to court to get a corporate trustee removed. The legal grounds for removing a trustee in most states are limited to:

— Willful negligence;
— Default or repudiation of the trust;
— Malfeasance (misconduct);
— Misfeasance (performing a lawful act in an unlawful manner);
— Dishonesty;
— Conflict of interest (this could include an inadvertent personal interest that's adverse to the interests of one or more beneficiaries);
— Failure to disclose accurate or material information;
— Taking unauthorized or excessive compensation, especially if it's not disclosed to the beneficiaries;
— Appropriating trust property for the trustee's own use.

A handful of states have lately made it easier for trust beneficiaries to move their accounts without going to court. California, Pennsylvania, Iowa, and the District of Columbia, for instance, reduce the burden of proof imposed on beneficiaries who want to change trustees in the event of a bank merger. In some of these cases, a beneficiary needn't prove theft or malfeasance; proof of mismanagement might suffice.

In any case, courts are a last resort, not a first resort, for removing a trustee, as the case of Louise W. Corbett suggests.

Louise Corbett's grandfather left her a trust that generated about 4 percent income annually. But after bank fees and charges, the return was just 2.85 percent. The trust was managed by two trustees: an individual and the Second National Bank of Boston, which after several mergers became the State Street Bank. Long dissatisfied with the management of the trust, Mrs. Corbett sent State Street Bank a letter in November 1991, asking permission to move her trust to

Florida, where she had moved from the Boston area. The bank denied her request. In February 1992 she asked the Massachusetts Banking Commission to intercede, but the commission declined, referring Mrs. Corbett to the probate court.

In April 1992 Mrs. Corbett hired Danielle deBenedictis, a Boston lawyer, who studied the trust document and discovered that it established an elaborate succession plan for future *individual* trustees but not for future *bank* trustees. This seemed to imply that Mrs. Corbett's grandfather had intended to enable her to remove trustees. Seizing on this point, lawyer deBenedictis informed State Street Bank that a lawsuit would be filed if the trust was not transferred. Three months later State Street Bank agreed to resign. From a list of acceptable banks provided by the Florida State Banking Commission, Mrs. Corbett chose Nations-Bank of Florida as the successor trustee. This new trustee's fees are only slightly lower, but the funds are now invested more aggressively.

Some investment advisers specialize in wresting control of personal trusts from unresponsive bank trustees and then transferring the responsibility to more cooperative successor trustees. The adviser's incentive is his hope that he'll get to serve as the trust's investment adviser, generating an asset management fee for himself every year that the arrangement continues.

One such adviser, Rob Rikoon of Rikoon Investment Advisers in Santa Fe, New Mexico, contends that "any trust can be moved," with or without going to court. Short of a lawsuit, he contends, threatening to hire an analyst who would independently review trust performance over the past several years and share the findings with the local media might cause the trustee to relinquish control with surprising swiftness. And if the matter does reach court, Rikoon maintains, most judges have no trouble with the practice of naming a successor trustee. At the worst, they may require that the replacement trustee reside in the same state as the original trustee, to keep the funds in-state.

WARNING: Just as a contingency-fee lawyer refuses to take a case he's unlikely to win, Rikoon declines to work with any family that seems hopelessly at loggerheads or insincere about moving a trust.

CHOOSING A SUCCESSOR TRUSTEE

Search for a trustee as you'd look for any professional adviser. Involve the entire family in the discussion. Ask for recommendations. Conduct personal interviews. Ask what services will be available and how the money will be managed. Then choose the candidate with whom you're most comfortable. Look for a trustee who's roughly your age. If you're looking at a bank or law firm, ask to see a younger associate. (If all the key people are elderly, you may run into problems if those people lose their ability to serve.) The important point, says Joshua Rubenstein, a New York trust and estate lawyer, is to "replace the corporate trustee with another independent trustee." (For more specifics on choosing a trustee, see *Part 1, page 69.* For advice on choosing personal advisers, see *Part 2, page 102.*)

If you're moving the trust from one bank trustee to another, here are some questions to ask the potential successor:

Will it accept a trust instrument that contains a trustee removal clause?

Will it administer a trust under an all-inclusive fixed fee contract?

Will it verify in writing that no referral fees will be paid?

Do the bank's management fees increase every two or three years? Does the bank invest the trust assets in its own proprietary mutual funds? (This could be a potential conflict of interest.)

Will it let an outside—presumably more aggressive—firm handle investments, with an appropriate reduction in fees?

DEALING WITH YOUR FELLOW BENEFICIARIES

Even if you have no complaints about your trustee, you may run into conflicts with your fellow beneficiaries whose needs or perspectives differ from yours.

For example, your brother may make a good living and prefer to see the trust principal grow for the benefit of his children, whereas you've had several medical catastrophes within your immediate family. You need maximum income from the trust and may even want to dip into the trust's principal assets, which would leave less for your brother in the long run.

Ideally, you should be able to appeal to his conscience: Would he rather be in your shoes, with a lifetime of medical bills to pay, than merely lose a piece of an inheritance he doesn't really need anyway?

This kind of dispute should never wind up in court, but often does. When beneficiaries sue each other, they usually say it's a matter of principle—but it's almost always a matter of money, or of psychological issues. However messy it may be to sue a trustee, intrafamily litigation is worse, and to be avoided at almost all costs. The enmity, publicity, and costs of a family court fight over money rarely justify the fight. In all events, talk—and then talk some more to try to avoid it.

One of the worst mistakes is to sue and then negotiate on the theory that bringing the lawsuit will help settle the matter. In fact, the opposite is often true: As positions become fixed, publicity mounts, discussions end, a court-designated guardian may be appointed immediately, and the toothpaste is forever out of the tube.

If you and your fellow beneficiaries can't resolve your differences, what are the alternatives?

◆ **Therapy or counseling.** An hour or two with a good therapist, family counselor, social worker, or psychologist—enabling two or more of you to confront your differences and work out the deep-seated psychological issues you may be unaware of—may be all that's necessary to straighten the issue out. If it requires 10 sessions, or even weekly sessions for a year or two, the process is still likely to be less expensive and more productive than a lawsuit. More private, too: A lawsuit hangs out your dirty linen for all the world to see.

Remember: A lawsuit is a scarring process; families that sue each other rarely get back together again, often to the regret of both sides. The billionaire Koch brothers of Topeka, Kansas, once shared living quarters when they were students at Massachusetts Institute of Technology. But beginning in 1982 they became embroiled in a series of lawsuits over control of the family's oil pipeline and ranching empire, Koch Industries. The two rival sets of brothers haven't spoken to each other since the late 1980s, not even at their mother's funeral in 1991.

Therapy is a healing process: You not only settle the issue at hand but also work out psychological approaches to dealing with similar conflicts in the future.

◆ **Arbitration.** The American Arbitration Association, other independent arbitrators, or "private" court systems like Judicate Inc. will, for a fee, hear your dispute privately and suggest a resolution. The cost is much less than that of a lawsuit—and again, it saves you the emotional burden of exposing your situation publicly. An arbitrator lacks coercive power to enforce her decision, of course. Usually arbitrators won't hear such a case unless the parties agree beforehand to abide by the arbitrator's decision. Check your phone book; the American Arbitration Association and Judicate have offices in many major U.S. cities.

◆ **If there's no rancor between you and other beneficiaries**—only an honest difference of needs, opinion, or
objectives—you might consider *splitting the trust* into
several trusts, each with a single beneficiary. This will
require amending or terminating the existing trust,
which can usually be accomplished legally if all beneficiaries and the trustee agree.

INHERITORS'
LIFESTYLE ISSUES

THE IMPORTANCE OF WORK

William Faulkner once observed that the only activity
people can perform for eight hours a day is *work*. That
may explain why people who don't have to work for a
living often seem unhappy—because there's nothing
else to do. You can't eat, read, exercise, play golf,
attend the theater, or make love for eight hours a day;
only work will fill up that time.

The solution is to find meaningful work for yourself
even if it's not financially necessary. If you don't need
or want a regular full-time job, many worthy causes
would welcome not only your donations but also your
time and talents. As the case of Stewart Mott suggests
(see *page 164*), what you derive from this arrangement
is a sense of purpose and connection to the rest of the
world. (See *Resources, pages 172–90*, for organizations
and publications that can help you make these connections.)

In the newsletter *More Than Money*, authors Anne
Slepian and Christopher Mogil suggest four approaches to meaningful work:

1 Develop a fulfilling career. A conventional career
offers a sense of confidence and the satisfaction of
earning one's own way in the world. On the other
hand, some inheritors feel guilty about taking a job
away from someone who may truly need the salary it
provides. If you succeed at a conventional career to the
extent that you're self-supporting, you'll then need to

WORKING INHERITOR: WILLIAM H. DANFORTH

AS THE GRANDSON of the founder of Ralston Purina, William H. Danforth II personally inherited some $35 million worth of stock in the giant food and feed products company. But he also inherited a driving compulsion "to accomplish something that would be lasting and that would leave the world a better place," as he once put it. He didn't turn his back on his wealth, but he did choose a career where his money was meaningless: medicine. His work as an internist and cardiologist led him into research at Washington University School of Medicine in his home town of St. Louis, where he made important discoveries in glucose metabolism and the energy supply of muscles.

Having demonstrated that he could succeed at a profession on merit alone, Danforth subsequently fell into a career that benefited from his wealth and background as well. When a bureaucratic feud erupted in the mid 1960s between Washington University's Barnes Hospital and the university's medical school, Danforth's unique combination of qualities—a calm bedside manner, family prestige, and corporate connections—made him the most promising mediator, even though he had no administrative experience at that point. (Indeed, he had never even had his own secretary or office.) In one leap, at age 40 Danforth went from a junior faculty member to vice-chancellor for academic affairs.

Danforth successfully resolved the feud between the med-

think about what to do with the inheritance you no longer need. (See the sidebar, *above.*)

2 Fund your own work. Many inheritors decide to live on their inheritance and work without a paycheck. They volunteer with existing organizations, work independently, or create their own organizations. But doing so means foregoing the validation of a regular salary and job title.

3 Make a job of managing your money. If you enjoy managing money, you can make your own inheritance a

ical school and the hospital so well that during the Vietnam War the university called on him again to mediate student anti-war protests. In 1971 he was named chancellor of the university—a post he thrived in for more than 20 years, at a time when most college chief executives were burning out after brief tenures. At the same time, as chairman of the huge Danforth Foundation, he pumped some $300 million into Washington University, until its endowment ranked among the nation's top 10. Yet throughout his years as chancellor, Danforth remained an unpretentious and approachable figure who drove an old car, wore 20-year-old suits, helped new students carry their bags to their rooms, and rejected even the most meager trappings of privilege, such as a reserved parking space or an unlisted phone number.

This combination—doctor, philanthropist, faculty member, and approachable administrator—earned him near-universal admiration in his home city for setting what one professor called "a humane tone for this campus." It also provided Danforth with an apparently ideal outlet for both his talents and his wealth. "He's just not interested in any place where he's not plugged into his community," his wife Ibby remarked in 1989. "He'd be miserable in a resort-type life. His philosophy is to serve the community, not to worry about his own future."

full-time job. Manage your own or your family's investments (perhaps drawing a salary). Or set up a foundation or charitable trust and become its administrator.

4 Become a social entrepreneur. Unlike conventional entrepreneurs, who start businesses to make money, social entrepreneurs launch businesses to fund worthy causes, or they launch worthy organizations themselves. But the line between the two isn't as clear as you'd think: Many successful business entrepreneurs eventually lose the kick they get from making money, at which point they look for ways to channel their entrepreneurial instincts into altruistic causes. In any case, these activities require business acumen and expert business advice.

THE REWARDS OF PHILANTHROPY

Many heirs find that a large inheritance removes much of the pleasure and meaning they derive from life in general and money in particular. But many find the antidote for this alienation in charitable giving.

Systematic philanthropy is a good idea for a more pragmatic reason as well: It reduces your tax burden. In most cases, charitable contributions of up to 50 percent of your adjusted gross income can be deducted from your income taxes.

Christopher Mogil and Anne Slepian, coauthors of *Welcome to Philanthropy*, offer this checklist for heirs who seek satisfaction from giving.

STOP WHATEVER MAKES GIVING UNSATISFYING. Some possibilities: Throw out direct mail appeals; remove your name from unwanted mailing lists; set limits for solicitations by phone canvassers; stop giving out of guilt or obligation.

CREATE A PROACTIVE AND FOCUSED PLAN TAILORED TO YOUR NEEDS AND INTERESTS. Choose a few areas related to your passions and concerns. Seek information about groups working in those areas. Choose your favorites and stick with them for many years. Make an annual giving schedule, so you do your giving on a regular basis—either monthly, quarterly, or annually. Earmark a percentage of your giving for spontaneous gifts to causes that move you. Reevaluate and revise your plan each year as needed.

MAKE MEANINGFUL PERSONAL CONNECTIONS TO THE GROUPS YOU FUND. Visit their projects. Volunteer to help. Make use of their services. Get to know the people involved (or give where you already know people).

GIVE IN WAYS THAT MAKE A REAL DIFFERENCE. Give a few large contributions rather than many small ones. Give to new or emerging charities rather than large, established ones. Give to groups less likely to receive mainstream support. Invite your friends to support your favorite causes. Give unrestricted funds for general operating expenses.

DEVELOP YOUR OWN SKILLS AS A SUPPORTER. Give fund-raisers a clear "yes" or "no" response, and follow through promptly on your pledges. Learn how different strategies (education, organizing, lobbying, direct action) help build social movements. Work on developing your own patience, compassion, and faith.

The philanthropist Stewart Mott adds these suggestions:

CONSIDER CREATING A PRIVATE FOUNDATION. If you don't yet have a specific philanthropic agenda, a foundation is a good place to park your money until you find a cause that inspires you. And if you're publicity-shy, a foundation's board of directors provides a convenient buffer between you and your applicants. Drawbacks: Although you're allowed to tax-deduct 50 percent of your income for charitable contributions, only 20 percent can be donated to private foundations. And the foundation's directors, even if you've handpicked them, may not always share your views.

MAKE YOUR CONTRIBUTIONS GENERATE OTHER CONTRIBUTIONS. Make pledges to match other people's donations to a cause, up to an amount you specify. This practice stimulates the organization to broaden its base of support instead of complacently leaning on you every year. And, of course, it generates greater contributions.

DON'T TOUCH YOUR PRINCIPAL. Giving away all your worldly goods to the needy may be a touching gesture, but in the long run the needy (and you, too) will be better served if you keep your assets and let them generate income for you to give away. (Thanks to Mott's astute use of investment advisers in his early years as a philanthropist, his assets and income grew, enabling his donations to grow from $230,000 in 1969 to more than $1 million in 1977.)

MINIMIZE YOUR TAXES. If you don't, the government will be the primary beneficiary of your largesse. The law permits you to deduct as much as 50 percent of your income each year for charitable contributions. Mott annually gives away—and deducts for tax purposes—the absolute maximum. (This strategy has its limits: The alternative minimum tax, designed to prevent high-income people from escaping taxation, removes certain deductions and imposes a flat income tax rate of 26 percent. But this is still lower than the top-bracket rate of 39.6 percent. Consult your accountant.)

AS MUCH AS POSSIBLE, MAKE GIFTS IN APPRECIATED STOCK RATHER THAN CASH. The law permits you to take a tax deduction for "in-kind" giving (stocks, art works, property, etc.) up to 30 percent of your gross adjusted income. If the value of your stock has risen, such donations can save you a lot on taxes. Suppose, for example, you bought 1,000 shares of CompuStuff at $10 a share—a total cost of $10,000—and the price has since risen to $15, increasing the total value of your investment to $15,000. You would like to donate that amount to your favorite charity, the Chicken Pox Foundation. If you sell the shares for cash, you'll have to pay a capital gains tax on the $5,000 profit, so you'll have less money to donate. But if you contribute the 1,000 shares outright, the Chicken Pox Foundation will receive a gift worth $15,000 and you'll be able to claim a $15,000 tax deduction, even though the shares cost you only $10,000.

IF YOU FIND A GOOD TAX DODGE, KEEP IT TO YOURSELF. Having avoided federal income taxes due to his contributions for three years in the mid 1970s, Mott boasted about his cleverness to so many people that

Congress passed the alternative minimum tax, aimed specifically at millionaires hiding behind loopholes. After paying no federal income taxes in 1973, 1974, and 1975, thanks to the alternative minimum tax, Mott paid $132,000 in 1976.

REMEMBER THAT IT'S ONLY MONEY. The best-laid plans and schemes may backfire; in such cases, grin and bear it. When Mott began large-scale giving in 1967, he embarked on an ambitious plan to donate each year more than 90 percent of his adjusted gross income to charity—a program which, if carried out for at least 8 out of any 10 years, would have entitled him thereafter to deduct up to 90 percent of his gross income for charitable contributions. But six years into the scheme, the law was changed: Today no one can deduct more than 50 percent for charitable contributions. "From a tax-deductible point of view," observed Mott's accountant, John Hodgkin, "those contributions made over the six years were wasted. Of course, Stewart doesn't think of them in those terms." (See the sidebar on *pages 164–65*.)

In a society that's at least theoretically a meritocracy, heirs have always experienced mixed feelings about inheriting large amounts that they didn't earn. Traditionally many have assuaged their guilt through traditional philanthropy: gifts to schools, colleges, hospitals, and cultural organizations. But in the Vietnam War era, a more rebellious generation of inheritors from some of America's most prominent families began gathering informally—at first just to commiserate, but later to use their inheritances to promote what they called "change, not charity." This "alternative philanthropy" movement blossomed in 1979 into the Funding Exchange, now a network of dozens of foundations, organizations, publications, and support groups in more than two dozen states (see *Resources, page 173*). Whether or not you agree with their goals— like support for battered women, abused children, the

HAPPINESS THROUGH PHILANTHROPY: STEWART MOTT

TWO CHARACTERISTICS distinguished Stewart R. Mott's entrance into the world in 1937: His father, Charles Mott, was (a) a founder and one of the largest stockholders of General Motors and (b) 62 years old. The double generation gap separating father from son, together with the elder Mott's standoffish manner, created an immense chasm between them. The father signed notes to his son, "Very truly yours, C. S. Mott"; when it came time for Stewart to learn to ride a bicycle, his parents hired someone to teach him; when Stewart, in his 20s, demanded a heart-to-heart talk with his father, the father scheduled an appointment at the General Motors Building in New York City and met Stewart across a conference table. As a bright but rebellious young man coming of age in the tumultuous 1960s, Stewart was rebuffed when he tried to get involved in his father's huge but conservative Mott Foundation.

It sounds like the classic formula for an unhappy heir. Yet by channeling his energies into philanthropy, Stewart Mott built an exuberantly rewarding life.

When he graduated from college in 1961, Mott had a $6 million nest egg and $850,000 yearly income from two trust funds of which he was an income beneficiary. While casting about for something to do, he discovered that his hometown of Flint, Michigan, lacked a Planned Parenthood branch—so he set one up. He obtained 500 birth-control kits from a manufacturer of contraceptives, passed out 40,000 flyers announcing their availability, hired a trailer, and distributed kits to passersby in low-income neighborhoods.

Planned Parenthood's national headquarters, impressed by Mott's missionary zeal as well as his checkbook, began dispatching Mott to other cities. Soon he was attending birth control meetings in London and Geneva and became one of Planned Parenthood's major supporters. From there it was a logical step to such causes as abortion law reform, the peace movement, and reform politics. In 1968 he moved to New

York to become a full-time philanthropist and fund-raiser.

From a Park Avenue penthouse covered with plants, vegetables, flowers, filing cabinets, desks, and piles of newspapers, Mott functioned as a one-man foundation—a tireless fundraiser, coordinator, consultant, board member, party-thrower, and editor of newsletters for causes he supported. Over the next 10 years he systematically gave roughly 50 percent of his adjusted gross income to charity—the maximum that could legally be deducted. He also gave more than $1 million to liberal political candidates (in the 1972 Presidential campaign he was George McGovern's largest contributor, giving $355,000). After these disbursements, he had barely $100,000 a year left to live on himself. But his work filled him with such a rewarding sense of purpose that he never took a vacation of more than one week.

"I always ask myself," he once told an interviewer, "'If I didn't have all this money, could I be earning the equivalent of what I spend on myself, or am I living beyond my hypothetical means?'" He concluded that as a professional fund-raiser he could probably draw a salary equivalent to the $100,000 or so he was living on by the end of the 1970s. "When I tell myself that, it reassures me that I'm not a leech on society."

His example subsequently inspired other heirs—like the fourth-generation Rockefeller cousins, milling heir George Pillsbury, and two sons of Seward Johnson (of Johnson & Johnson)—to challenge their families' conservative foundations in order to support progressive causes like ecology and feminism.

"My definition of success," Mott once remarked, "is finding what you most want to do, so that your work eight hours a day corresponds to your physical and emotional needs. That connection is much more important than wealth, power, or prestige. I come across far too many people in their 20s and 30s who are floundering because they haven't made that connection. I'm happy beyond words that I have."

homeless, the disabled, and gays and lesbians—these groups may offer useful services for dealing with your inheritance. They also offer numerous cases of heirs who defined themselves through creative philanthropy.

On his 21st birthday in 1970, the milling heir **GEORGE PILLSBURY JR.** gave most of his $400,000 inheritance away to organizations aimed at changing the status quo. He subsequently launched the Haymarket People's Fund in Boston and was an early financial supporter of food co-ops, the leftish *Ramparts* magazine, and documentary films on social issues. He subsequently became development director of the Jobs With Peace campaign, spending much of his time conducting conferences and counseling for wealthy inheritors, aimed at steering them toward socially responsible giving and investing. When Pillsbury Company was sold in 1989, he gave his $125,000 capital gain to the Funding Exchange, the national umbrella organization of local alternative foundations, which he serves as a consultant. Says his sister, Los Angeles filmmaker Sarah Pillsbury: "He's given his whole life to philanthropy."

OBIE BENZ, heir to two fortunes—a Delaware baking company and the Daimler-Benz motor car company—was fresh out of Middlebury College in 1972 when he started San Francisco's Vanguard Foundation, the first of his generation's alternative philanthropies set up by children of the rich "to give grants to programs that could not get money anywhere else." Vanguard funded some of the nation's first rape crisis centers and shelters for battered women; it also helped fund medical rights for the poor, lesbian rights, peace causes, and Hispanic cultural activities. In 1978 Benz launched the Pacific Alliance to fund antinuclear activities on the West Coast; it subsequently expanded nationally. His MUSE Foundation threw an antinuclear rock concert that raised $450,000 and was celebrated in the 1980 film *No Nukes*.

HELEN HUNT HENDRIX, next youngest daughter of Texas oilman H. L. Hunt, divided much of the 1980s between her household of six children and her Hunt Alternatives Fund, which supports low-income community groups, homeless rights, and the mentally ill in New York and Dallas. She helped create the Dallas Women's Foundation and was instrumental in establishing nationwide "Women Helping Women" coalitions between rich and poor women. Had she not become a social activist, she once remarked, "I would be miserable, leading a golden-handcuffs kind of life."

ALIDA ROCKEFELLER, daughter of philanthropist John D. Rockefeller III, was a founder of the Headwaters Foundation in Minneapolis, which she described as seeking to fund "social change at the grass-roots level" and to encourage leadership and self-esteem among the poor. One example: She supported radio station KILL, owned and operated by Oglala Indians on the Pine Ridge reservation in South Dakota.

CHARLES COLLINS, a great-grandson of Oscar Mayer, founder of the meat-packing company, learned at 16 that he would come into an inheritance. "I dreaded the whole idea," he later told *The New York Times*. "My father told me I need never work, but he hoped I would."

To assure that he would work, in 1986 Collins gave virtually all of his $300,000 to George Pillsbury's Haymarket People's Fund. Subsequently he supported himself on a modest salary from the Institute for Community Economics, a nonprofit organization that operates the nation's largest loan fund for low-income housing.

"My biggest worry was the bad effect this might have on my family relations, and I simmered inside," he remarked. "But I was able to talk it through during long walks with my father." When the Funding Exchange gave him its first Robin Hood Award in

1989, Collins responded, "All I did was the moral equivalent of finding a wallet on the street and returning it to its owner."

A CLOSING THOUGHT: WE PASS THIS WAY BUT ONCE

You've heard it said that a chain is only as strong as its weakest link. The world, like your family, didn't begin with you, nor will it end with you. Each of us is merely a link in the fragile but enduring chain that binds our tenuous lives to humanity's ancient past and its unknowable future. That's a humbling thought, but also a comforting one: It means that you bear an awesome responsibility, but it also means that you're a more important player on this planet than you may have thought.

"The blossom cannot tell what becomes of its odor," wrote the 19th-century minister Henry Ward Beecher, "and no man can tell what becomes of his influence." Your inheritance, no matter how large or small, represents the accumulation of thousands of human relationships stretching backward to the dawn of time. So take good care of it. You owe that much to your ancestors who worked so hard to put you where you are today. And you owe that much to your descendants, who'll punch your ticket to immortality long after you've departed.

This book has provided some of the basic tools for coping with that transition. If you need more help, you'll find many additional resources in the pages that follow. The effort is well worth your time and energy. Transferring a legacy—whether it's material, intellectual, or spiritual—from one generation to the next may turn out to be the most important thing you ever do.

Good luck!

RESOURCES

THIS BOOK OPENED by observing that many guide-books explain how to plan your estate or write your will, but virtually none tell you how to be on the receiving end. This is true. But it's not true that you have no place else to turn. A wealth of professional advisers, organizations, publications, and inheritors' support groups all exist to address your needs. What follows is a selective guide to some of these resources.

SUPPORT GROUPS

INHERITORS' SUPPORT GROUPS

Heirs Inc. Founded in 1991; 2,500 members, nearly all trust beneficiaries unhappy with the terms of their trusts. Publishes newsletter; lobbies legislators; keeps abreast of news, strategies, and legal matters; publicizes problems of beneficiaries; holds an annual conference. Standish H. Smith, founder and president. Box 292, Villanova, PA 19085 (610-525-4442). Voice mail: 610-527-6260. Web site: www.marpleinfo.com/heirs.

The Inheritance Project. Offers a confidential phone interview designed to help heirs break through the taboo against talking about their money. Katherine Gibson, cofounder. P.O. Box 933, Blacksburg, VA 24063-0933 (540-953-3977). Web site: inheritance-project.com.

Resourceful Women. Offers a variety of classes, support groups, and conferences for women with inheritances of $25,000 or more. Programs in 11 cities. Issues a variety of publications, including a selective guide to professional advisers. Judy Bloom, executive director. Thoreau Center for Sustainability, Bldg. 1016, P.O. Box 29423, San Francisco, CA 94129-0423 (415-561-6520). Fax: 415-561-6462. E-mail: distaff@rw.org. Web site: www.thoreau.org/TENANTS/RW.html.

RELATED SUPPORT GROUPS

Most of the following groups were created by wealthy inheritors seeking to change or reform the system that enriched their families. Among these groups, support and advice for inheritors are an important by-product, but the primary agenda is fostering social change.

The Comfort Zone Collaborative. Umbrella organization for groups of young people with wealth working for social change. Partners include Boston Women's Fund, Haymarket People's Fund, Impact Project, Peace Development Fund, United Black and Brown Fund, Youth on Board. Publishes *Money Talks; So Can We,* a resource guide for people in their 20s. Cost: $15 for for-profits, $12 for individuals and nonprofits. Lynne Gerber and Tracy Hewat. C/o PDF, Box 1280, Amherst, MA 01004 (413-256-3806, ext. 225).

Co-op America. A marketplace for educating consumers and businesses in socially conscious directions. Provides some useful basic materials on financial planning and philanthropy. 1612 K St. NW, Suite 600, Washington, DC 20006 (202-872-5307). Web site: www. coopamerica.org/

Funding Exchange. A national network of alternative foundations committed to funding social change. Holds educational programs for inheritors; also offers donor-advised grant-making services. 666 Broadway, Suite 500, New York, NY 10012 (212-529-5300).

Haymarket People's Fund. A social-change foundation that holds workshops and conferences for inheritors. Its programs cover the personal, technical, political, and philanthropic aspects of taking charge of inherited money. 42 Seaverns, Jamaica Plain, MA 02130 (617-522-7676). Web site: www4.homecom.com/ host1039/hay/haymark.html.

The Impact Project. Nonprofit organization that specializes in encouraging young heirs and other young rich to engage their money and talents to support social-change philanthropy. It offers individual coun-

seling, organizing, workshops, and the quarterly publication *More Than Money*. 21 Linwood St., Arlington,
MA 02174 (781-648-0776). E-mail: mtmnews@aol.
com. Web site: www.qcfurball.com/impact.

Other women's funds. Two local women's self-help
groups offer conferences for women to increase their
financial literacy. Workshops cover topics like financial planning, socially responsible investing, and
women's economic development. **Boston Women's
Fund,** 376 Boylston St., Boston, MA 02116 (617-375-
0035). **Maine Women's Fund,** Box 5135, Portland, ME
04101 (207-865-1004).

INHERITANCE AND
WEALTH ADVISERS

Individual Consultants. Branch of the Impact Project
providing consultants who specialize in working with
wealthy people on emotional and practical challenges
of managing wealth. Ask for a list of professionals.
21 Linwood St., Arlington, MA 02174 (781-648-0776).
E-mail: mtmnews@aol.com.

PERSONAL AND TECHNICAL MONEY ISSUES

Tom Batterman, president, Vigil Asset Management
Group, 401 N. Fifth Ave., Wausau, WI 54401 (715-848-
8110). E-mail: tbatterman@vigilasset.com. Web site:
www.vigilasset.com. Financial planner who works with
inheritors.

Lu Bauer, 196 Gray Rd., Falmouth, ME 04105 (207-797-
0466). Accountant.

Olivia Boyce-Abel, 1003 Smith Grade, Santa Cruz, CA
95060 (408-469-0223). Specializes in family lands.

Cynthia D. Coddington, vice president/director, Financial Planning Group, David L. Babson & Co., 1 Memorial Dr., Cambridge, MA 02142-1300 (617-761-3859).
Fax: 617-225-3801.

Ellen Deacon, 4501 Spruce St., Philadelphia, PA 19139
(215-662-5261).

David Diesslin, Diesslin & Associates, 303 Main St., Fort Worth, TX 76102-4067 (817-332-6122). Financial planner with a psychologist wife.

Jeffrey Feldman, Ph.D., Rochester Financial Services, 890 Winton Rd. S., Rochester, NY 14618 (716-442-7580). Financial planner.

Nancy Frank, Frank Advisory Services, New York, NY 10021 (212-535-3832). E-mail: infrank@worldnet.att.net. Financial planner and an inheritor herself.

Deena Katz, Evensky, Brown, Katz & Levitt, 241 Sevilla Ave., Coral Gables, FL 33134 (305-448-8882). Financial planner.

Brent Kessel, CFP. Abacus Financial Planning, 1535 Sixth St., Suite 101, Santa Monica, CA 90401 (888-4-ABACUS). Fax: 310-457-3137. E-mail: abacusbk@earthlink.net. Financial planner.

Jennifer Ladd, 245 Main St., Apt. 206, Northampton, MA 01060 (413-585-9709).

Judy Lau, Lau & Associates, 300 Bellevue Parkway, #120, Wilmington, DE 19809 (302-792-5955). Financial planner who works with those who have inherited wealth.

Warren Mackensen, Mackensen & Co., 31 Forest Drive, Hampton, NH 03842 (603-926-8085). Financial planner and an inheritor himself.

Christopher Mogil and Anne Slepian, 21 Linwood St., Arlington, MA 02174 (617-648-0776). *See also* The Impact Project under "Related Support Groups."

Raj Pillai, Financial Fitness Network, Inc., 6175 SOM Center Rd., Cleveland, OH 44139 (440-248-4984). E-mail: advisor@unbiased.com.

Marc D. Pressman, Pressman Financial Consulting, 641 South Wesley Ave., Oak Park, IL 60304 (708-524-0444). Fax: 708-524-0430. E-mail: mpress@ pipeline.com. Financial planner, formerly with the trust department of Bank of Boston.

Roger Pritchard, 1514 McGee Ave., Berkeley, CA 94703 (510-527-5604). Specializes in community investment.

Rob Rikoon, Rikoon Investment Advisors Inc., 3878 Old Santa Fe Trail, Santa Fe, NM 87505 (505-989-3581). Fax: 505-983-8086. E-mail: rikoon@$l.geis.com. Investment adviser who specializes in wresting control of trusts from uninterested bank trustees and transferring control to a more cooperative successor trustee.

Barbara Steinmetz, 111 Anza Blvd., Suite 208, Burlingame, CA 94010-1932 (650-401-3800). Fax: 650-401-3830. E-mail: steinplan@aol.com. Financial planner and an inheritor herself.

Rosemary Williams, 115 Puritan Rd., Fairfield, CT 06430 (203-255-3961). Financial planner.

FAMILY BUSINESS CONSULTANTS

James Gallagher, 3636 Paradise Dr., Tiburon, CA 94920 (415-435-3406).

International Skye, Peter White, principal. 2900 M St. NW, Suite 200, Washington, DC 20007 (202-625-6128). Fax: 202-625-6204. E-mail: peterw@skye.com. Professional consulting firm specializing in inheritors' issues, such as family businesses, family leadership, succession planning, and philanthropy. Holds seminars and institutes.

The Le Van Co., P.O. Box 10, 101 West St., Black Mountain, NC 28711 (828-669-0131). Managing director Gerald Le Van, a former lawyer, has written books on family business issues; functions as intermediary between heirs and parents; and was formerly a regent of the American College of Trust & Estate Counsel.

Joel Solomon, 2006 20th Ave. S., Nashville, TN 37212 (615-297-5550).

PHILANTHROPIC CONSULTANTS

Meg Gage and Katrin Verclas, Ottinger and Careth Foundations, 256 N. Pleasant St., Suite 2, Amherst, MA 01002 (413-56-0349).

Tracy Gary, Community Consulting Services/Strategic Philanthropy, P.O. Box 428, Ross, CA 94957 (415-461-5539).

Virginia Hubble, 283 Second St. East, Sonoma, CA 94576 (707-938-8248).

Iva Kaufman, 900 West End Ave., Suite 7B, New York, NY 10025 (212-864-1892).

Doug Malcolm, 70 Wellwood Rd., Portland, ME 04103 (207-772-3245).

Bill Somerville, 12121 Preservation Park Way, Oakland, CA 94612 (510-645-1890).

Charles Terry, Rockefeller Financial Services, 30 Rockefeller Plaza, Room 5600, New York, NY 10112 (212-649-5600).

PSYCHOLOGICAL ISSUES

Judy Barber, 1515 Fourth St., Suite B, Napa, CA 94559 (707-255-6254). Fax: 707-255-6254. Also publishes *Family Money. See also* "Publications."

Joanie Bronfman, 1731 Beacon St., Apt. 517, Brookline, MA 02146 (617-739-0548).

Sarah LaSaulle, 1452 26th St., Santa Monica, CA 90404 (310-453-5421).

John L. Levy, 842 Autumn Lane, Mill Valley, CA 94941 (415-383-3951). A psychologist specializing in problems of inheritors; comes from a well-to-do family himself.

Money Strategies Inc., Myra Salzer, principal; 1919 14th St., Suite 319, Boulder, CO 80302 (303-444-1919). Financial planning firm that works exclusively with inheritors. One partner handles money management, the other handles psychological issues. Conducts seminars and workshops; also provides family office services for individuals who lack their own family offices.

Jessie O'Neill, 8940 N. Upper River Rd., River Hills, WI 53217 (414-351-6534).

Dennis Pearne, 9 Alexander Ave., Belmont Centre, MA 02178 (617-484-0013).

Thayer Wills, 1730 Englewood Ct., Lake Oswego, OR 97034 (503-245-1288).

ORGANIZATIONS

Consumer Federation of America. Its insurance group can provide an analysis of your insurance needs. Enclose a stamped, self-addressed envelope. 1424 16th St. NW, Suite 604, Washington, DC 20036 (202-387-6121).

Council on Foundations. Major philanthropic support organization. Among other events, it holds an annual family foundation conference. Also publishes various guides on creating and running a foundation. 1828 L St. NW, Suite 300, Washington, DC 20036 (202-466-6512). E-mail: infoserv@cof.org. Web site: www.cof.org.

Family Firm Institute. Association of some 1,000 family-business consultants, financial planners, attorneys, and psychologists specializing in wealth transfer and preservation. Ask for directory of members or consult its Web site: www.ffi.org. 12 Harris St., Brookline, MA 02146 (617-738-1591). Fax: 617-738-4883.

Family Office Exchange. Advises high-net-worth families on uses of a family office to further a family's legacy and investment goals. Sara Hamilton, president. 137 N. Oak Park Ave., Suite 310, Oak Park, IL 60301 (708-848-2030). Fax: 708-848-2131.

Franklin Research and Development Corp. Oldest and largest firm specializing in socially responsible investing. Publishes two newsletters, *Franklin Research's Insight* ($225 per year) and *Investing for a Better World* ($29.95); 711 Atlantic Ave., Boston, MA 02111 (617-423-6655). Web site: www.frdc.com.

HALT: An Organization of Americans for Legal Reform. Not-for-profit legal reform organization dedicated to simplifying legal affairs. Publishes consumer advice books on legal issues and lobbies for legal reforms and for simplification of forms and procedures for wills, divorces, and trusts. 1612 K St. NW, Suite 510, Washington, DC 20006 (202-887-8255; also 888-FOR-HALT). Fax: 202-887-9699. Web site: www.halt.org.

The Social Investment Forum, 1612 K St. NW, Suite 650, Washington, DC 20006 (202-872-5319). A professional association of socially responsible financial advisers and institutions. E-mail: info@social invest.org. Web site: www.socialinvest.org.

National Association of Personal Financial Advisors (NAPFA). Organization of consultants who work on a fee-only basis (as opposed to a percentage of assets). Can provide a directory of members and other materials (such as questions to ask before hiring a financial planner). 355 W. Dundee Rd., Suite 200, Buffalo Grove, IL 60089 (847-537-7740). Fax: 847-537-7722. E-mail: info@napfa.org. Web site: www.napfa.org.

FAMILY THERAPY

American Association for Marriage and Family Therapy. 1133 15th St. NW, Suite 300, Washington, DC 20005-2710 (202-452-0109). Fax: 202-223-2329. Web site: www.aamft.org. Ask for its directory of clinical members.

American Board of Examiners in Clinical Social Work. 21 Merchants Row, Boston, MA 02109 (800-694-5285). E-mail: abe@abecsw.org. Web site: www.abecsw. org.

National Association of Social Workers. 750 First St. NE, Suite 700, Washington, DC 20002-4241 (202-408-8600). Ask for its register of clinical social workers. Web site: www.naswdc.org.

National Council on Family Relations. 3989 Central Ave. NE, Suite 550, Minneapolis, MN 55421 (612-781-9331; also 888-781-9331). Ask for its list of certified family life educators. Web site: www.ncfr.com.

National Registry of Certified Group Psychotherapists. 25 East 21 St., New York, NY 10010 (212-477-1600).

PUBLICATIONS

The American Benefactor. P.O. Box 57440, Boulder, CO 80322-7440 (800-856-8659). Quarterly magazine aimed at philanthropists; also deals with other issues concerning transfer of wealth. Web site: www. AmericanBenefactor.com.

Chronicle of Philanthropy. P.O. Box 89, Marion, OH 43306 (202-466-1200). Leading mainstream philanthropy journal. Web site: www.philanthropy.com.

Family Money: A Commentary on the Unspoken Issues Related to Wealth. 1515 Fourth St., Suite B, Napa, CA 94559 (707-255-6254). Fax: 707-257-0582. Thrice-yearly newsletter with much useful information, published by Judy Barber, a specialist in the psychology of money.

Fiduciary Fun. Heirs Inc. ($85 per year); Box 292, Villanova, PA 19085 (610-525-4442). Voice mail: 610-527-6260. Web site: marpleinfo.com/heirs. Newsletter for trust beneficiaries published by Heirs Inc.

The Green Money Journal. West 608 Glass Ave., Spokane, WA 99205 (509-328-1741; also 800-318-5725). Web site: www.greenmoney.com. Newsletter and Web site provide information and resources on socially responsible investing.

More Than Money. 2244 Alder St., Eugene, OR 97405 (541-343-2420; also 800-255-4903). E-mail: impact@efn.org/~impact. Web site: www.efn.org/~impact. A quarterly publication of The Impact Project (*see also* "Related Support Groups") that explores the psychological, spiritual, and practical impact of wealth on inheritors' lives. Ask for Issue No. 3, "Money, Work and Self-Esteem," which deals with work issues for people who don't need a paycheck. Issue No. 9 deals with "Money and Children," especially inheritance issues. $35.00 per year; single-copy back issues are $7.00.

BOOKS

GENERAL RESOURCE GUIDES

Money Talks; So Can We. A resource guide for inheritors in their 20s. Published by The Comfort Zone Collaborative, c/o PDF, Box 1280, Amherst, MA 01004 (413-256-3806, ext. 225). Cost: $15.00 for for-profits, $12.00 for individuals and nonprofits.

Taking Charge of Our Money, Our Values and Our Lives. A comprehensive 64-page guide to more than 350 publications and organizations related to money and wealth; revised 1998. Published by The Impact Project, 21 Linwood St., Arlington, MA 02174 (617-648-0776). (For more on The Impact Project, see "Related Support Groups.")

TRUSTS AND ESTATES

Gerald Condon and Jeffrey Condon, *Beyond the Grave: The Right and Wrong Way of Leaving Money to Your Children.* Toronto: HarperBusiness, 1996, $14.00 (800-331-3761).

Norman Dacey, *How to Avoid Probate, Updated!* Riverside, New Jersey: Macmillan, 1990, $16.95. Provides do-it-yourself forms for wills and living trusts.

The Easy Way to Probate: A Step-By-Step Guide to Settling an Estate. Washington, D.C.: HALT, 1994, $10.00 plus $2.00 shipping. How to handle the probate process. Available from HALT: An Organization of Americans for Legal Reform, 1612 K St. NW, Suite 510, Washington, DC 20006 (202-887-8255; also 888-FOR-HALT).

Stephan Leimberg and others, *Tools and Techniques of Estate Planning.* Best of the estate planning books. Cincinnati: National Underwriter Company, 1995, $42.50 (800-654-2227).

David S. Magee, *Everything Your Heirs Need to Know: Your Assets, Family History & Final Wishes.* Chicago: Dearborn Financial Publishing, 1995, $19.95. Some advice, but mostly a workbook filled with forms to fill out with vital information for parents or spouses to leave for their heirs.

Passing Wealth Along to Our Children: Emotional Complexities of Estate Planning, $13.50. A 25-page monograph about the emotional complexities of creating trusts and wills; $12.00. Available from The Inheritance Project, P.O. Box 933, Blacksburg, VA 24063-0933 (540-953-3977). Web site: inheritance-project.com.

Theresa Meehan Rudy, Kay Ostberg, and Jean Dimeo, *Your Guide to Living Trusts and Other Trusts: How Trusts Can Help You Avoid Probate and Taxes.* Useful manual published in 1994 by HALT, 1612 K St. NW, Suite 510, Washington, DC 20006 (202-887-8255; also 888-FOR-HALT); $10.00 plus $2.00 shipping charge.

Standish H. Smith, *The Heirs Personal Trust Handbook.* Guide for dealing with practical issues such as creating and terminating a trust, troubleshooting trust performance, and changing trustees, by the founder of the Heirs Inc. organization; 1997, $85.00. Available from Heirs Inc., Box 292, Villanova, PA 19085.

Using A Lawyer . . . And What To Do If Things Go Wrong. Washington, DC: HALT, 1990, $8.95 plus $2.00 shipping. Explains how to shop for a lawyer and get the most out of her. Available from HALT, 1612 K St. NW, Suite 510, Washington, DC 20006 (202-887-8255; also 888-FOR-HALT).

Wills: A Do-It-Yourself Guide. Washington, D.C.: HALT, 1992, $8.95 plus $2.00 shipping. Enables you to draft a valid will without an attorney. Also discusses estate planning, living wills, trusts, and durable powers of attorney. Available from HALT, 1612 K St. NW, Suite 510, Washington, DC 20006 (202-887-8255; also 888-FOR-HALT).

PSYCHOLOGY OF INHERITANCE

Michael Alexander, *How to Inherit Money.* Toronto: HarperBusiness, 1997, $20 in paperback. The author was executor for two large inheritances he received. The book is mostly psychological but also contains some financial advice.

Barbara Blouin, Katherine Gibson, and Margaret Kiersted, *The Legacy of Inherited Wealth: Interviews With Heirs.* Blacksburg, Virginia: Trio Press, 1995, $17.95. Interviews with 17 inheritors, exploring the emotional aspects of inherited wealth. The authors, inheritors themselves, are co-founders of The Inheritance Project. Available from P.O. Box 933, Blacksburg, VA 24063-0933 (540-953-3977). Web site: inheritance-project.com.

Joanie Bronfman, *The Experience of Inherited Wealth: A Social-Psychological Perspective.* Ann Arbor, Michigan: UMI Dissertation Information Service, 1987. A painstaking examination of how wealthy heirs experience their situation.

The Inheritor's Inner Landscape: How Heirs Feel. Monograph published by the Inheritance Project, exploring emotional challenges heirs may face in coming to terms with their wealth; $13.00. Available from P.O. Box 933, Blacksburg, VA 24063-0933 (540-953-3977). Web site: inheritance-project.com.

Gerald Le Van, *Transforming Business Families.* Published by the author, a former estates lawyer now consulting for family businesses. Contains some good sections on inheritance issues; $17.95. P.O. Box 10, 101 West St., Black Mountain, NC 28711 (828-669-0131).

Olivia Mellan, *Money Harmony: Resolving Money Conflicts in Your Life and Relationships.* New York: Walker, 1995, $9.95. A useful resource on understanding money dynamics in personal relationships and how to make them work better.

MONEY MANAGEMENT AND PERSONAL FINANCE

Janet Bamford et al., *The Consumer Reports Money Books: How to Get It, Save It and Spend It Wisely.* New York: Consumer Reports Books, 1997, $29.95. A readable reference to basic financial planning and money management.

Marshall Blume, Jeremy J. Siegel, and Dan Rottenberg, *Revolution on Wall Street: The Rise and Decline of the New York Stock Exchange.* New York: Norton, 1993, $27.50. Clear primer on how stock markets work and how investing has changed over the years.

Emily W. Card and Adam L. Miller, *Managing Your Inheritance.* New York: Times Business/Random House, 1996, $15.00. Web site: www.randomhouse.com.

Emily W. Card, *The Ms. Money Book.* New York: E.P. Dutton, 1990 (out of print).

The Co-op America Handbook for Financial Planning. Washington, D.C.: Co-op America, 1998, $6.00. Good basic guide to financial planning, aimed at young inheritors (202-872-5307).

Joe Dominguez and Vicki Robin, *Your Money or Your Life: Transforming Your Relationship With Money and Achieving Financial Independence.* New York: Viking, 1993, $12.95. A guide to financial independence, simple living, and greater personal fulfillment.

Nancy Dunnan, *Dun and Bradstreet Guide to Your Investments.* New York: HarperCollins, 1998, $19.95; updated annually. A thorough resource on the full range of investment options.

Lyn Fraser, *Understanding Financial Statements.* Englewood Cliffs, New Jersey: Prentice-Hall, 1997, $34.67.

Martin Kuritz, John Sampson, and David Sanchez, *The Beneficiary Book.* New York: Viking, 1996, $29.95.

Deanne Stone and Barbara Block, *Choosing and Managing Financial Professionals.* Booklet guiding novice investors in selecting a good financial adviser. Published by Resourceful Women (*see* "Inheritors'

Support Groups.") San Francisco: Resourceful Women, 1994, $12.00 (415-561-6520).

Eric Tyson, *Personal Finance for Dummies*. San Mateo, California: IDG Books Worldwide, 1994, $19.99. Comprehensive reference book that explains personal finance in simple terms.

MEANINGFUL WORK

Nancy Anderson, *Work With Passion: How to Do What You Love for a Living*. San Rafael, California: New World Library, 1995, $12.95. Advice and exercises to help the reader identify and find fulfilling employment.

Richard Nelson Bolles, *The 1998 What Color Is Your Parachute?* Berkeley, California: Ten Speed Press, 1997, $16.95. Updated annually. Classic self-help vocational planning manual, delightfully written and lavishly illustrated.

Inheritors and Work: The Search for Purpose. Inheritance Project, 1996, $16.50 postpaid. P.O. Box 933, Blacksburg, VA 24063-0933 (540-953-3977). Web site: inheritance-project.com.

Anthony Mancuso, *How To Form a Nonprofit Corporation*. Berkeley, California: Nolo Press, 1998, $39.95. Provides specific regulations for each state. (*Note:* Since laws constantly change, these must be double-checked.)

Marsha Sinetar, *Do What You Love, The Money Will Follow: Discovering Your Right Livelihood*. New York: Paulist Press, 1989, $11.95. Classic book on how to find work you love, by one who succeeded.

CONTRIBUTING YOUR TIME

Susan Angus, editor, *Invest Yourself*. New York: The Commission on Voluntary Service and Action, $8.50. Directory of volunteer service opportunities (out of print).

Jeffrey Hollender, *How to Make the World a Better*

Place: 116 Ways You Can Make a Difference. New York: Norton, 1995, $13.00. Well-informed catalogue of 116 ways to protect the environment, reduce hunger, invest money responsibly, etc.

Jerald Jampolsky, *One Person Can Make A Difference: Ordinary People Doing Extraordinary Things.* New York: Bantam, 1992, $10.00 (out of print). True stories of people who have followed their hearts and taken action to improve the world.

Marlene Wilson, *You Can Make A Difference: Helping Others and Yourself Through Volunteering.* Boulder, Colorado: Volunteer Management Associates, 1993, $12.95. A personal guidebook to contributing time to worthy causes.

SOCIALLY RESPONSIBLE INVESTING

Jack A. Brill and Alan Reder, *Investing From the Heart: The Guide to Socially Responsible Investments and Money Management.* New York: Crown Publishers, 1992, $20.00; $12.00 in paperback (out of print). A comprehensive and accessible beginners' guide. Presents an overview of ethical money management; also provides detailed analyses of hundreds of specific stocks, bonds, mutual funds, and limited partnerships.

Peter Kinder, Steven Lyderberg, and Amy Domini, *Investing For Good: Making Money While Being Socially Responsible.* New York: HarperBusiness, 1994, $13.00 (out of print). A primer for investors on how to screen companies according to a variety of environmental and social concerns.

Peter Kinder, Steven Lyderberg, and Amy Domini, *The Social Investment Almanac.* New York: Henry Holt, 1992, $50.00. More than 40 essays from 50 professionals on many aspects of social investing, including community development, shareholder action, portfolio management, and social venture capital. Available from 270 Congress St., 7th floor, Boston, MA 02210.

Susan Meeker-Lowry, *Invested in the Common Good.* Philadelphia: New Society Publishers, 1995, $16.95. Offers hundreds of suggestions as to how ordinary people can invest money or time in progressive causes.

PHILANTHROPY

Joan Flanagan, *Successful Fundraising: Complete Handbook for Volunteers and Professionals.* Chicago: Contemporary Books, 1993, $18.95.

Douglas K. Freeman and Lee Hausner, *A Founder's Guide to the Family Foundation.* Council on Foundations, 1996, $25.00. A 34-page booklet that offers basics on starting and running a foundation. Available from Council on Foundations, 1828 L St. NW, Suite 300, Washington, DC 20036 (202-466-6512).

Tracy Gary and Melissa Kohner, *Inspired Philanthropy: Creating a Giving Plan.* Berkeley: Chardon Press, 1998, $20.00.

Robin Hood Was Right: A Guide to Giving Your Money for Social Change. The Funding Exchange, updated 1997, $9.00 (out of print). A resource for inheritors interested in donating money toward progressive social-change causes. Available from the Funding Exchange, 666 Broadway, Suite 500, New York, NY 10012 (212-529-5300).

Christopher Mogil and Anne Slepian, *We Gave Away a Fortune.* Philadelphia: New Society Publishers, 1992. Case histories of 16 inheritors who devoted their energies and money to worthy causes. $18 postpaid from The Impact Project, 2244 Alder St., Eugene, OR 97405.

Christopher Mogil and Anne Slepian, *Welcome to Philanthropy.* National Network of Grantmakers, updated 1997, $25.00. A 50-page resource guide to social-change giving. Describes conferences for wealthy inheritors, donor-advised accounts, and dozens of other resources. Available from the publisher at 1717 Kettner Blvd., Suite 110, San Diego,

CA 92101 (619-231-1348). E-mail: nng@nng.org.

Claude Rosenberg Jr., *Wealthy and Wise: How You and America Can Get the Most Out of Giving.* Boston: Little Brown & Co., 1994, $24.95. Suggests how to evaluate your income and net worth in deciding how much money to give away.

Allan J. Samansky, *Charitable Contributions and Federal Taxes.* Charlottesville, VA: Michie Co., 1993, $105.00 (out of print).

SELECTED ARTICLES

MAGAZINES

Katherine Zoe Andrews, "Philanthropy's Workhorse" (charitable remainder trusts), *American Benefactor,* Spring 1997, pp. 29–32.

April Bernard, "Passing the Bucks," *Town & Country,* Oct. 1992, p. 120.

Emily W. Card, "Expert Advice: What a Financial Planner Can and Can't Do for You," *Ms.,* Oct. 1986, pp. 40–43.

Emily W. Card, "Planning Your Parents' Estate," *Working Woman,* Aug. 1992, p. 39.

Carol Curtis, "A Matter of Trusts," *Financial World,* Jan. 8, 1991, pp. 50–52.

John Dizard, "The New Family Office," *American Benefactor,* Summer 1997, pp. 43–46.

Carolyn T. Geer, "Is Your Trust Well-Placed?" *Forbes,* Jun. 16, 1997, pp. 190–94.

Davidson Gigliotti, "Pity the Poor Heir," *Sarasota* magazine, Mar. 1996, pp. 64–65.

Philip Herrera, "Here Come the Wealth Consultants," *Town & Country,* Mar. 1997, p. 115.

Donald Jay Korn, "Revolt of the Trust-Fund Babies," *Financial Planning,* Feb. 1996, pp. 39–46.

Margaret Opsata, "Trust Buster" (Rob Rikoon), *Dow Jones Investment Advisor,* Apr. 1997, pp. 66–70.

Mary Rowland, "A Trustee to Trust," *Modern Maturity,* Nov./Dec. 1996, pp. 58–59.

Laura Saunders, "In Roth We Trust," *Forbes*, Apr. 20, 1998, pp. 466–68.

Laura Saunders, "In Whom We Trust," *Forbes*, Jun. 24, 1991, pp. 200–203.

Laura Saunders, "King Lear, updated," *Forbes*, Mar. 9, 1998, pp. 216–17.

Ellyn Spragins, "A Cautionary Tale" (trusts), *Town & Country*, Oct. 1992, pp. 128–29.

Laura Walbert, "In Charity We Trust," *Town & Country*, Oct. 1992, p. 126.

William D. Zabel, "Thy Will Be Done?" (estate planning), *Town & Country*, May 1991, pp. 123–30; Jun. 1991, pp. 111–18.

PAPERS

John L. Levy, "Coping With Inherited Wealth," $10.00, 22 pages. Available from the author, a psychologist, at 842 Autumn Lane, Mill Valley, CA 94941 (415-383-3951).

John L. Levy, "Trusts vs. Trust." Nine pages; discusses the human side of creating trusts. Available from the author *(see above)*.

Robert B. Wolf, "Defeating the Duty to Disappoint Equally: The Total Return Trust," *Real Property, Probate and Trust Journal*, Spring 1997, pp. 45–102.

NEWSPAPERS

"An Heir Finds a Loophole to Move a Trust," *The New York Times*, Jun. 25, 1994; p. 38.

Andrée Brooks, "Beneficiaries Complain of Rules and High Fees," *The New York Times*, Jul. 3, 1993, p. 32.

L. Stuart Ditzen, "Furor over Family Fortunes: Heirs Want Some Say on Their Trusts," *Philadelphia Inquirer*, Mar. 10, 1991; p. 1-A.

Katherine Fraser, "Trust Reform Group Clamors for Freedom to Switch Banks," *American Banker*, Dec. 22, 1995, p. 1.

Katherine Fraser, "Group Asking Banks to Quit Trusteeships if Beneficiaries Upset," *American Banker,* Feb. 14, 1996; p. 8.

Michael deCourcy Hinds, "Modern Crusade: Plight of the Rich," *The New York Times,* Jul. 2, 1991; p. A-10.

Iidacq, Jeanne, "Trust Clients Sue over Sweep Fees," *American Banker,* Feb. 12, 1992, p. 3.

Margaret A. Jacobs, "Row over Hanes Estate Cuts Family Ties," *The Wall Street Journal,* Dec. 18, 1996, p. B-1.

Kathy Kristof, "Care in Setting Up Family Trusts Can Head Off Problems," *Los Angeles Times,* Jun. 9, 1996, p. D-2.

Gerald Le Van, "Intergenerational Accord Eases Estate Planning," *National Law Journal,* Dec. 9, 1996, p. B-12.

B.J. Roche, "Trust Beneficiaries Losing Trust in Big Buyers of Local Banks," *Boston Globe,* May 28, 1996, p. 43.

Jan M. Rosen, "Some Breathing Room to Change Trustees," *The New York Times,* Jul. 9, 1994, p. 34.

Dan Shingler, "Roadway Heirs Allege Advisors Squandered Family Trusts," *Crain's Cleveland Business,* Jun. 20, 1994, p. 1.

Kathleen Teltsch, "Founded by Idealists, Group Thrives on Need" (Funding Exchange), *The New York Times,* Jan. 30, 1990, p. A-18.

GOVERNMENT AGENCIES

Social Security Administration (800-772-1213). Automated 24-hour service. Web site: www.ssa.gove.

Veterans' Affairs (800-827-1000). To obtain burial information. Web site: www.va.org.

GLOSSARY

Administrator. A court-appointed figure who disposes of an intestate estate. His or her duties are identical to those of an executor; the only difference between the two titles concerns whether the decedent left a will.

Annuity trust. A charitable remainder trust that provides the donor a fixed annual income.

Assets. Money and real or personal property owned by an individual or an organization.

Benefactor. In relation to trusts, the person who sets up the trust and provides the funds. Synonym for a *creator, donor, grantor, settlor,* or *trustor.*

Beneficial interest. The right to enjoy or profit from property held in trust; the person with the beneficial interest is the *beneficiary.*

Beneficiary. The person or persons for whose benefit a trust is created. Usually (but not always) refers to the persons who receive the income from the trust, as opposed to those who receive the principal after the trust expires.

Bequest. The gift of personal property left in a will.

Bond. A monetary guarantee that, should a trustee steal trust funds, compensation will be awarded up to the amount of the bond.

Bypass trust. A trust typically created by married couples to contain property in order to exclude it from the estate of the surviving spouse. The surviving spouse receives income from this trust but not the principal. Also called a *credit shelter trust,* a *family trust,* or a *non-marital trust.*

Capital gains. Growth in value of an asset, such as stocks or real estate. Within a trust, capital gains are treated as part of the corpus, not as income.

Charitable lead trust. A trust that donates to a charity income from trust assets while reserving the assets for later distribution to other beneficiaries.

Charitable remainder trust. A trust that pays income from trust assets to the donor or beneficiaries while reserving the assets for later contribution to a charity.

Charitable trust. A trust created for the benefit of a charity. The two most common types are the charitable lead trust and the charitable remainder trust.

Community property. Property acquired during marriage that was not a gift to or inheritance of one spouse or specifically kept separate.

Contingent interest. Interest in a property that is dependent on some future event (such as a college graduation or a marriage) as opposed to the passage of time. Opposite of *contingent interest.*

Corpus. The body, or principal, of a trust's holdings. In trust and tax law the corpus is distinguished from the income that the corpus generates.

Court trust. Synonym for a *testamentary trust* or *will trust.*

Creator. The person who creates a trust by providing money or property for it. Synonym for a *benefactor, donor, grantor, settlor,* or *trustor.*

Credit estate tax. A state tax on the assets of someone who has died. It applies only in some states, and only to estates that are required to pay federal estate taxes. Instead of paying double estate taxes, the estate pays a credit estate tax, which rebates part of the federal estate tax owed back to the state.

Credit shelter trust. Synonym for a *bypass trust.*

Creditor. A person or corporation to whom money is due.

Death tax. Synonym for an *inheritance tax* or *estate tax.*

Disclaimer. The act of refusing to accept an inheritance.

Donee. The recipient of a gift, trust, or power left in a trust; also the beneficiary of a trust.

Donor. The person or corporation who gives a gift to or confers a power on another. Also refers to the creator of a trust. Synonym for a *benefactor, creator, grantor, settlor,* or *trustor.*

Durable power of attorney. A short legal document in which an individual authorizes someone else (usually a close relative or trusted friend) to manage his affairs in the event of incapacity. *Durable* means that it survives the signer's becoming incompetent. A *general* durable power of attorney means it applies to all the signer's affairs, as opposed to a *limited* power of attorney, which deals with only a specific matter, such as health care or finances.

Estate. All the property, real or personal, that a person owns.

Estate tax. A type of death tax based on the decedent's right to transfer property (not a tax on the property itself). Also called a *death tax* or an *inheritance tax.*

Executor. The person (or institution) named in a will or by a court to execute or carry out the terms of the will and settle the decedent's estate. (Female: executrix.)

Family pot trust. A trust that pools assets for distribution to several children based on need.

Family trust. Synonym for a *bypass trust.*

Federal estate tax. A tax assessed against the assets of a person who has died if the value of the taxable assets exceeds the estate tax exclusion limit (which will rise in annual steps from $625,000 in 1998 to $1.2 million in 2006).

Fiduciary. A person in a position of trust and confidence whose duty is to act for the benefit of another. A trustee and an executor act as fiduciaries.

Fiduciary control. The right granted to another party (usually a bank, trust company, or trustee) to engage in trades and transfers once money has been placed with them.

Future interest. Interest in property that can't be possessed or enjoyed until a specified date or event (such as a 21st birthday) occurs. Opposite of *present interest.*

Generation-skipping tax. A provision of the 1986 federal income tax reform law that forces taxation at each generation that property is passed down. Previously, grantors could bequeath property directly to their grandchildren and thus skip one generation's worth of estate tax on that amount.

Generation-skipping trust. A trust designed to skip one generation of estate taxes because the trust leaves the principal to the grantor's grandchildren, not the children. See *generation-skipping tax* above.

Gift. A voluntary lifetime or at-death transfer of property, made without compensation.

Gift tax. A tax on transfers of property made within the donor's lifetime without consideration, or for less consideration than the property is worth.

Grantor. In relation to trusts, the person who sets up the trust and provides the funds. Synonym for a *benefactor, creator, donor, settlor,* or *trustor.*

Grantor trust. A living trust in which the grantor maintains enough control over the assets so that the trust income received is taxed to the grantor, not to the trust or the trust's beneficiaries.

Gross estate. Property owned by a decedent at death, before estate taxes and administrative expenses have been deducted.

Guardian. A person or corporation appointed by a court to handle the affairs or property of another who is unable to do so because of incapacity.

Heir. A person or corporation designated to inherit property from someone who has died.

Income beneficiary. A beneficiary of a trust who receives only the income generated by the trust assets.

Index fund. A mutual fund that invests in a diversified group of stocks reflecting some broadly based index, like the Standard & Poor's 500 Index. It enables a small investor to match the performance of the market as a whole.

Inheritance tax. The tax imposed on property received by beneficiaries from the estate of a decedent. Also called a *death tax* or an *estate tax.*

Insurance trust. A trust that owns and manages a life insurance policy and designates its beneficiaries.

Inter vivos trust. A trust created to take effect during the life of the trust grantor. It can be either revocable or irrevocable. Synonym for a *living trust*.

Intestacy. The state of dying without a valid will.

Intestate. Having died without leaving a valid will.

Irrevocable trust. A trust that, once created, cannot be changed or terminated by the grantor. Consequently, an irrevocable trust is treated as a separate entity for legal and tax purposes.

Joint tenancy with right of survivorship. A form of ownership in which property is equally shared by all owners and is automatically transferred to the surviving owners when one of them dies.

Kiddie tax. A provision of the 1986 federal income tax reform law that taxes all annual income above $1,000 paid to children under age 14 at their parents' rate.

Life estate. A property right limited to the lifetime of its holder, often income from an estate. This right can't be passed to an heir.

Living trust. A trust set up and put into effect while its creator is still living. It is a vehicle that enables elderly people to manage their own assets jointly with a co-trustee, who can take charge in the event of the grantor's death or incapacity. Such a trust is revocable. Synonym for an *inter vivos trust*.

Living will. A document (separate from a will) in which a person expresses a wish that his or her life not be prolonged by artificial life-support systems if his or her medical condition becomes hopeless.

Nonmarital trust. Synonym for a *bypass trust*.

Pay-on-death account. Synonym for a *Totten trust*.

Per capita. A will or trust distribution plan that requires that all of the grantor's living descendants, regardless of generation, receive an equal share of the grantor's estate. Opposite of *per stirpes*.

Per stirpes. A will or trust distribution plan that requires that descendants of a deceased beneficiary, as a group, inherit equal shares of the amount the deceased beneficiary would have received had he or she lived. (For example, if you die before your father, your children would receive equal shares of your inheritance.) Opposite of *per capita*.

Perpetuities, rule against. A law preventing property from being transferred through trusts from one generation to another indefinitely.

Personal property. Movable property, as opposed to land, buildings or other things attached to land.

Pour-over. A provision in a will that distributes money or property to a trust that already exists.

Power of appointment. Power given in a trust to a donee to dispose of the grantor's property. A power of appointment can be general or limited. If it's general, the donee can give the property to anyone, including himself. If it's limited, the property must go to someone other than the donee or the donee's estate.

Power of attorney. A short document appointing another individual to manage one's affairs. Can be general (applying to everything at all times) or durable (applying to specific matters and/or at specific times).

Present interest. The right to use property immediately. Opposite of *future interest* or *contingent interest*.

Principal. Property in a trust. Synonym for *corpus*.

Probate. The legal process of establishing the validity of a deceased person's last will and testament. The term commonly refers to both the process and laws for settling an estate.

Probate court. A special court designed to deal exclusively with estates.

Q-TIP (Qualified Terminable Interest Property) Trust. A trust that qualifies for the marital deduction and postpones payment of any estate taxes owed until both spouses have died. The surviving spouse receives trust income for life but has little or no legal right to the trust's principal.

Real property. Immovable property, such as land, buildings, and other things attached to land.

Remaindermen. The persons who will receive the body of a trust after it expires.

Removal clause. A provision in a trust describing how and for what reasons a trustee may be removed.

Res. The subject matter or contents of a trust or will. See also *corpus* and *principal.*

Residual beneficiary. A person who receives remaining property that hasn't specifically been given away in a trust or will. The term also refers to the person who receives property only after the original beneficiary has died.

Residuary trust. Synonym for a *bypass trust.*

Revocable trust. A trust that can be changed after its creation by the grantor—unlike a testamentary trust, which is irrevocable once the grantor dies. Because the grantor remains in control, a revocable trust receives no special tax benefits.

Rule against perpetuities. See *perpetuities, rule against.*

SEC. The U.S. Securities and Exchange Commission, created by Congress in 1934 to regulate the stock and bond markets.

Section 2503(c) trust. A trust that allows a grantor to make gifts of $10,000 a year to the trust for the future benefit of minor children without the grantor incurring gift taxes.

Settlor. Someone who creates a trust. Synonym for a *benefactor, creator, donor, grantor,* or *trustor.*

Spendthrift clause. A provision included in some trusts that prohibits the beneficiary from giving or selling to others the beneficiary's rights to the trust's assets or income.

Standby trust. A living trust that takes effect if a grantor becomes ill or incapacitated, or dies. The grantor's assets are transferred to the trust and managed by the designated trustee.

Successor trustee. The person who takes over the rights and responsibilities of an original trustee.

Tenancy by entirety. A form of spousal ownership in which property is equally shared and automatically transferred to the surviving spouse. As long as both spouses are living, ownership of the property can be altered only by divorce or mutual agreement.

Tenancy in common. A form of jointly owning property in which each person's share passes to his or her heirs or beneficiaries, but the ownership shares need not be equal.

Testament. Synonym for a *will*.

Testamentary trust. Any trust created under a last will and testament. Unlike a living trust, a testamentary trust is irrevocable—that is, it cannot be changed after death (except through extensive legal contortions). Synonym for a *court trust* or *will trust*.

Testate. Having died leaving a valid will.

Totten trust. A revocable trust created by the owner of a bank account for the future benefit of another. Synonym for a *pay-on-death account*.

Trust. A legal entity created to hold and manage property for the benefit of others (beneficiaries).

Trust B. Synonym for a *bypass trust*.

Trust income. Generally the interest, dividends, and rents that the trust corpus produces.

Trustee. The fiduciary who holds trust property and administers it for the benefit of the trust's beneficiaries.

Trustor. Someone who creates a trust. Synonym for *benefactor, creator, donor, grantor,* or *settlor*.

Unitrust. A charitable remainder trust that provides the donor a fluctuating annual income based on investment performance.

Unlimited marital deduction. A provision that allows a spouse to transfer all property to his or her spouse without federal estate tax.

Vest. To grant immediate and full ownership rights.

Will. A legal document in which a person declares how he would like his property disposed of after his death. Synonym for a *testament*.

Will trust. Synonym for a *court trust* or *testamentary trust*.

INDEX

ABOUT BLOOMBERG

Bloomberg L.P., founded in 1981, is a global information services, news, and media company. Headquartered in New York, the company has nine sales offices, two data centers, and 80 news bureaus worldwide.

Bloomberg Financial Markets, serving customers in 100 countries around the world, holds a unique position within the financial services industry by providing an unparalleled combination of news, information, and analytic tools in a single package known as the BLOOMBERG® service. Corporations, banks, money management firms, financial exchanges, insurance companies, and many other entities and organizations rely on Bloomberg as their primary source of information.

BLOOMBERG NEWS℠, founded in 1990, offers worldwide coverage of economies, companies, industries, governments, financial markets, politics, and sports. The news service is the main content provider for Bloomberg's broadcast media, which include BLOOMBERG TELEVISION®—the 24-hour cable television network available in ten languages worldwide—and BLOOMBERG NEWS RADIO™—an international radio network anchored by flagship station BLOOMBERG NEWS RADIO AM 1130℠ in New York.

In addition to the BLOOMBERG PRESS® line of books, Bloomberg publishes BLOOMBERG® MAGAZINE and BLOOMBERG PERSONAL FINANCE™.

To learn more about Bloomberg, call a sales representative at:

Frankfurt:	49-69-920-410	San Francisco:	1-415-912-2960
Hong Kong:	852-977-6000	São Paulo:	5511-3048-4500
London:	44-171-330-7500	Singapore:	65-438-8585
New York:	1-212-318-2000	Sydney:	61-29-777-8686
Princeton:	1-609-279-3000	Tokyo:	81-3-3201-8900

ABOUT THE AUTHOR

Dan Rottenberg is the author of seven books, including *Finding Our Fathers* and *Revolution on Wall Street.* He has written articles for major magazines such as *Forbes, The New York Times Magazine,* and *Town & Country,* and has been a columnist for the *Philadelphia Inquirer* since 1978.